The Scars Beneath Her Smile

By

Chyna Kendle Rose

Dedication

I'd like to dedicate this book to everyone in the world who has suffered abuse in any form. No abuse should be down played. Abuse is Abuse! Everyone deserves to be treated with love and respect.

I'd also like to dedicate this book to my angels, visible and Invisible.

To my visible Angels: My son Jamin, you've given me the strength and courage to weather any storm that has come my way since the day you were born. It was a dire need to push and pray my way through, because I have you to take care of. My goal in this life is to make sure that you are proud of me-as your mother. I love you more than life itself!

My family: Wil, Tishia, Lashea, Kim, Tiffany, & Phree. You all are amazing for encouraging me to put this book into motion, pushing me to keep writing when I felt that my story wasn't good enough. Reading, editing, brainstorming etc, you all helped me give life to my story. I am forever grateful.

Last but not least: To my Loving God, thank you for planting this gift inside of me and helping me realize how special it is. Without you, I'm nothing. With you, I can achieve great things!

Prologue

Autumn is a free spirited yet misjudged girl challenging the odds of being the stereotypical "black girl" in Buffalo, New York, while overcoming the small-town mentality that constantly threatens her growth and success. After enduring years of neglect and abuse at the hand of her teenage parents and those close to her, Autumn was in search of several important things: direction, peace of mind and purpose.

Through the power of prayer and determination she honed her purpose and began putting a plan in motion to escape her past and attain her destiny. Relocating to Atlanta, Georgia, Autumn set out on a journey to find out who she was outside of the "sex symbol" her home town labeled her to be. She dreamed big and Hotlanta was the perfect place for a new beginning.

Find out what happens when Autumn is exposed to the "Dirty South" and gets caught up in a tangled web of lust, manipulation and unadulterated drama. Will she become a product of her environment or will she uncover the diamond in the rough?

Chapter 1

Roots

Conceived to the song "Juicy" sung by Mtume in a backyard of an abandoned house, Autumn was born in Spring of 1983 to a handsome- tall, slim, Mocha skin toned Father with big beautiful cocoa brown eyes and a smile that could light up a room- charmer named Mike-Red who was a jack of many trades - a hustle man as the streets would call it. Mike had the gift of gab, which meant he could sell water to a well. While driving taxicabs in the city, he hustled, street gambled and even sold merchandise out of the trunk of his car. This young slickster had the perfect gig that landed him a mass clientele, picking up customers and servicing their drug needs.

His ladylove and mother of his children, Aleyah, who stood 5'2, Caramel skin toned with Strawberry Blonde and Dark brown hair, green slanted eyes and full pink lips. She was built like a 'brick house' 34c-cups, small waist and a fat round ass.

She had the remedy to make all his troubles disappear. She was his safe haven. Mike always came home to a hot meal and warm bed - she was attentive to his needs and always had his back.

Aleyah complemented his style in many ways, keeping up her appearance and playing her position well. She loved Mike just as much as he loved her. They came from two totally different backgrounds, a classic case of the good girl who loves the bad boy.

Mike showered Aleyah with love by giving her access to everything she wanted; there were shopping sprees, new cars, fly apartments, and his money. They were ignorant adolescents in love and exploring life carefree. But the street life is bittersweet, with the easy fast money came serious problems.

There was never a dull moment in their world; from the love wars between them (because they were too young to honor monogamy) to being on the run from druglords. Autumn didn't appreciate being exposed to a daring life at such an innocent age. She lived in constant fear that someone would intentionally hurt her family. This made her feel trapped and distrusting of others. Mike's advice and actions were a relentless reminder for Autumn to always watch her back. There was also a hunger that lived inside of her. She wanted to be in a different environment. She decided not adapt to the same lifestyle as her parents and was determined to change her identity and go somewhere she could spread her wings and fly.

Chapter 2
Aleyah's Branches

Aleyah's Grand-Papa was born in the early 1900's during the Jim Crow era. He was a tall, dark, handsome, and charming railroad contractor in New York. He later traveled south in hopes of gaining an opportunity for better working conditions and higher pay. He met his wife after relocating to Gadsden, Alabama, who at the age of thirty-four, passed away from a heart attack, leaving behind five children - three girls (one being Aleyah's mother) and two boys.

Sweet-Ma, Aleyah's mother, was a Southern belle raised with Christian faith and the epitome of a woman. She was polite, always smiled and spoke with a gentle tone. Her cooking skills would make anyone fall in love. She believed in taking good care of her family and she taught her daughters the importance of loyalty, strength, family, faith, and the true meaning of womanhood.

Papa-J, Aleyah's father, was the complete opposite of her mother in terms of personality. He was direct and outspoken; there was no sugar coating with him. He was also a man of intellect and wisdom, a man who had always been an excellent provider and protector of his family, he had an reputation in the streets for choking a man to death with his bare hands if he or his family were disrespected. Her father was the epitome of a man; he enjoyed working with his hands, hunting and fishing. His family never went hungry. He taught his two daughters the importance of independence, responsibility and the meaning of what a real man looks like.

Aleyah's parents were married for over 50 years. As parents they were a great pair; she was a homemaker who went to church every Sunday and he was the prototypical alpha male whose hard work set the tone for their family. Together they planted seeds, grew vegetables, fruits, and flowers. Their family structure was built on faith, love, strength and a special bond created at the dinner table. As in any family though, children have rebellious tendencies. Aleyah was not immune to this, she ended up taking an interest in a bad boy and dropped out of high school in the tenth grade. All in the name of love.

Chapter 3
Mike Sees Red

Mike's background was much darker and very deep...

Mike-Red was the product of a "dysfunctional family." With both parents addicted to cocaine, Mike and his siblings often had to fend for themselves. Their father's addiction grew so powerful that he ended up abandoning his family. This left Mike's mother to raise four children (three sons and one daughter) on her own in one of the roughest, poorest neighborhoods in Buffalo. It was an environment mired in poverty, drug dealers, drug addicts, prostitution, and a lack of opportunity.

They lived in the projects, an old run-down apartment building that had become unmanageable. It got so bad that eventually all of the utilities were shut off. The majority of the tenants moved out but Mike's family remained. For them affordable rent was more important for a family of five living on one income than worrying about the oppressive surroundings.

Mikes mother, Lola, worked long hours as a registered nurse to make ends meet. She also had a habit to maintain which meant her children were left unattended and responsible for themselves most of the time.

One night as Mike came home after hanging out with his friends; he entered the building and headed up the stairs to their 5th floor apartment. He ran through the dark halls that were filled with addicts, the smell of urine, and rats.

As he reached the 3rd floor, a junkie came out of one of the abandoned apartments. "Hey you!" the Junkie said. "Come here, I need you to help me with something..." Mike paused out of fear and shouted "What do you want?!" He grabbed Mike by the wrist and asked "You got some blow?"

"Blow?" Mike asked. "I'm not a dealer. I'm just a kid, let go of my arm!"

"I know you have some, hook me up!" the Junkie begged. He began searching Mike's body in hopes of finding what he was looking for. "Come on man, I'll suck yo dick!"

Mike tried his best to break away from the crazed junkie, but there was no way a 9 year old boy could muster the strength to overcome a grown man who was on a coke trip. The junkie pulled Mike's pants down grabbed his penis, massaged it, then dropped to his knees to perform oral sex. Mike fought until the end with tears covering his face, he screamed out for help, but no one heard his cries, his voice echoed throughout the long halls leaving marks along the walls. When the junkie realized that Mike didn't have what he was looking for, he hit Mike over the head with a bottle knocking him unconsciousness.

Mike awoke hours later with a busted lip, blood gushing from his head and his pants around his ankles. When he stood to his feet, he immediately noticed that his body functioned differently. With every step he took, the walls seemed to be closing in on him, but he was determined to make it back home where he would feel safe.

Lola had just come in from work when Mike staggered through the door. Lola immediately noticed there was something wrong with her son and rushed to his side. They cried in unison as Mike tried his best to explain how he had been violated. Lola was horrified as the words left her child's mouth. She immediately called 911. Hours went by before a unit finally arrived to file a report. By that time only God knew where the abuser had gone. The police didn't seem to be concerned with the importance of the matter. Injustice had been served to another black family in the ghetto. Lola couldn't help but feel overwhelmed with conviction. She had to live with the fact that she was partly to blame for Mike being abused and there was nothing she could do to remove the scars from his heart. This traumatic experience shook the entire family to its core. It also set the tone for madness to come.

Insomnia filled the walls in their home, sending the struggling family over the edge. Lola had no clue of how to console her children during such a tough time. She herself needed encouragement moving forward but had no one turn to for support, so she made herself numb to the world by popping muscle relaxers she took from the hospital where she worked, a few shots of gin, and several lines of cocaine.

Mike was restless. The constant replays of the nightmare were overwhelming. He felt alone because there was no one to love him through the hurt or help him understand his feelings. This left him confused and angry at the world. Mike wanted to get even for all that he'd endured, the abuse, his father leaving their family struggling and watching his mother drown in depression everyday was killing him. Lola would only laugh or sleep after she had taken a drink from the bottles she kept at the bottom of the fridge or in the cabinets. Mike wondered if he would feel better and rest better by doing the same.

One night after Lola passed out, he crept to the kitchen and grabbed the bottle marked "Wild Irish Rose" he took a sip of the happy juice in hopes of magic results.

Cringing at the harsh taste and burning sensation in his chest, he sipped a few more times. At that moment he became a rebel as he sat on the kitchen floor to captivate its effect. The room began to spin a little, which made him giggle because he couldn't stand up straight to walk to his bedroom. Mike thought to himself, *it's true, the happy juice works, I can laugh again.* He laid in his bed giggling until he fell into a deep sleep for the first time in a long while. That began the chain of bad habits to come for Mike.

Growing up in the projects, it was common to see people standing on the corners or on their porches sipping from brown paper bags filled with alcohol. Getting drunk and high was a daily activity. To blur the vision of all of the poverty, filth, and lower quality of living, Mike soon adapted to his surroundings like a chameleon. The deprivation of love and attention drove him to the streets to fill the voids in his life.

He had a strong desire to be a part of something where he could feel important. He'd heard from friends that joining a gang could give him that love and support he was seeking. Soon, he began hanging around with the local thugs to see if he would fit in. In the hood, to be initiated into a gang, one has to prove his loyalty by "walking the walk and talking the talk", so

Mike began smoking weed, loitering on the corners and drinking 40oz beers to prove that he was down for whatever. Next, the crew challenged Mike to commit a robbery. They paired him with Joe, another young boy under the initiation process, and supplied the props for the stick up. Mike and Joe were each given a gun, which were stolen and had bodies on them, some duct tape, and were instructed to wear all black everything.

Joe and Mike set out on their first venture. As they rode through the city, they presumed the best place to hit would be the downtown area where the middle class people lived. They figured they were sure to find something impressive to take back to the crew. They parked on Chippewa Ave. and sparked up a joint as they watched people shopping and dining out. Finally they spotted their victims, it was a couple in their mid-30's, dressed nicely and jeweled up leaving a restaurant. The couple was holding hands, laughing, walking, and recapping their evening. The boys were nervous but excited as they stepped out of the car to hide beside a bush. Once the guy went to open the car door for his lady, the two boys popped from behind the bushes, dressed in all black with ski masks covering their faces. Before the couple knew what was happening, they were staring at two guns. "Give me your wallet, your jewelry and the keys to the car Mr. Romance!" yelled Joe. "Don't move or make a sound!" yelled Mike.

The guy was so nervous he couldn't grab his wallet fast enough while his lady was crying and shaking. Mike nervously checked the scene to make sure that no one was watching. Joe grew impatient and hit the man upside his head with the gun, knocking him out instantly. The lady began to scream hysterically. "Help me get him in the trunk!" yelled Joe.

"What the fuck dude? The trunk?" snapped Mike.

"Do you want to be a part of the crew or not? I'll spread the word that you punked out!"

Mike grabbed the duct tape out his pocket, placing it over the man's mouth and wrapped his hands. As they were putting the guy inside the trunk the lady ran away. Mike saw her, but didn't mention it to Joe. His conscience had kicked in, leaving him filled with remorse, but it was too late, he was already in too deep. Once they closed the trunk, sirens began blaring. The boys hopped inside the car and drove off. "Hurry up, the sirens are getting louder!" yelled Mike. "Relax man, we're good!" Joe yelled back.

"So, what are we going to do with the dude in the trunk?" Mike asked. "We'll find a spot to dump him. His ass is out cold, so we can check to see what else he's holding. That nigga looks like he's loaded. Check the glove compartment for credit cards."

The boys pulled into a dark alleyway behind a warehouse, popped the trunk and took the man's watch, wedding ring, cash, credit cards, and his social security card. They sat him near a dumpster and drove off in his car. They were so hyped up about pulling off their first crime, they laughed all the way back to the crew.

Mike had earned his street credit and place with the gang that night. He felt untouchable now that he was part of "The Stick Up Kids" squad.

With Mike having a high yellow skin tone and being slick, his homeboys nicknamed him "Dirty Red" (aka "Mike-Red"). The young thugs celebrated by drinking a few bottles of Hennessey, firing up some blunts and calling a few girls over. Mike ended the night feeling powerful for the first time in his life and nobody could take that feeling away. His new influences helped shape his rebel history.

Since Mike-Red and Joe pulled such a slick move by bringing back the car, their new hustle was to steal cars and sell them to chop shops. Successful in their new life of crime, they were making $500 a pop for each car they brought in. Mastering their hustle in such a short time, he and Joe started bringing in five to ten cars a week. This continued for several years. These young thugs created an illegal business that was in high demand. They had verbal contracts with chop shops all over the city. The shops would place orders for certain makes, models and parts of vehicles that the boys would deliver.

One night, the boys were making a delivery to an older gangster named Nino. He invited them to smoke a joint while he counted out the paper he owed to them.

"Ya'll young boys make big money stealing cars?" asked Nino.

"Hell yeah, we make plenty dough," said Mike as he and Joe slapped hands and laughed with pride. "That's chump change," said Nino. "I'll teach you how to make a few thousand dollars in a matter of hours. You niggas will be balling in no time. If you're interested in living the good life follow me..."

Nino, was a drug distributor (aka "The Connect") who was well known around the town for having the best cocaine/heroin/weed... you name it, Nino sold it. He also had a reputation for knocking off his competition.

Mike-Red and Joe followed Nino to the back.

"Let me school you young bloods to the rules of the drug game. Watch your back, because niggas are hungry out here in these streets and they'll do whatever it takes to get that money. You've got to hold down your block. Don't let anyone except for the po-po run you off. Keep your strap close at all times in case you have to body a nigga. Next, as long as you have a quality product, the fiends will shop with you. The scheme of it is to lure them in with the potent shit. After their second purchase you can give them the watered down product, that'll keep them chasing that very first high and they'll keep coming back for more. In simple terms, it would be like shooting fish in a barrel. Last, but not least, DON'T get caught! If you do, you have to take one for the team. Loyalty is everything in this game, you *never* turn your back or snitch on your squad. Snitches get bodied, that includes your family too!"

Inside the warehouse (chop shop) the gangsters had an entire production line set up. In one room there were thugs counting money, smoking weed and shooting dice. In another room there were eight guys; two were mixing and cooking cocaine and heroin, three other guys were breaking down the product and distributing it into small glass containers. The last three were posted near the exits holding guns. Their job was to watch and make sure there was no pinching off the stash. Mike-Red and Joe took one look around at the money and decided they wanted in.

It didn't take Mike-Red long to build up his clientele.

With the gift of gab and a strong rep from stealing cars, he was set. His favorite motto was: *I can sell water to a well*. He still lived at home with his mother and siblings, so stacking his money was easy. He was quickly becoming hood rich, which made the decision to drop out of school that much easier. His mentality was that there was nothing school could teach him to bring in the type of money the streets were offering. At that point he had just given up on his education, the streets was now his teacher and he was eager to learn. Mike had developed great skills in gambling and hustling, it was fast easy money and he was in love with his new profession.

Chapter 4
Bad Boy meets Girl, Girl the Perfect Woman

It was a hot summer day when Mike-Red and his older brother Alain were driving around the town trying to find some trouble to get into. When they turned on Sycamore Avenue thcy saw a girl walking down the street dressed in a colorful tank top and short shorts that cupped her juicy ghetto booty. After following her in the car for a few blocks and making flirty comments to get her attention, Mike couldn't resist the opportunity to get out of the car and introduce himself to the young beauty. They exchanged names and phone numbers before the girl told him she had to go because she was late for her summer job. Mike stared at her completely mesmerized by her beautiful green eyes and full-lips, he wasn't ready for the moment to end. "If you were my girl, I'd take care of you. You would never have to work because I would give you everything that your heart desired."

The girl blushed, revealing her high cheek bones, then asked if he was being sincere. The look in his big soft cocoa brown eyes answered her question. She never made it to work that day and they were inseparable from that point on. That pretty young thing was Aleyah.

Mike truly adored her, there was something about her that made his heart skip a beat and he wasn't shy about sharing his feelings to the world. She gave him a sense of comfort, her spiritual background made it natural for her to encourage him, giving him the confidence to do anything his put his mind to. She would massage his head as she whispered *you are the greatest, most powerful man to walk this earth* into his ear, making him feel untouchable before he walked out of the door for the day/night. And the way their bodies intertwined when they made love was astonishing, her warm, tight, wet walls felt like magical little fingers rubbing his penis. He also loved that her pussy was sweet like berries, he couldn't resist tasting her, making love to her gave him the strength of ten men. Aleyah gave him something to believe in, he had never experienced such a great love. He made a vow to never allow this love to leave his life. For that reason, Mike showered her with gifts, jewelry, clothes, shoes, etc. and assured her that there was more to come.

Aleyah was head over hills for Mike as well. Given that she had been raised in a strict Christian home, Mike provided a life of excitement for her. The way he walked, like he had a monster in his pants. The way he talked, like he knew everything in the world, whatever he had, he made you feel like you needed to have it, it would improve the quality of your life. And he was great company, he could make you laugh so hard that you pee'd your pants. With him life was an adventure. He took her places and showed her things she'd never seen. Mike opened her eyes to the world outside the church.

To add the cherry on top, his thick Love fit like a Glove inside her pussy, he'd always stroke it a few times, then pull out to French kiss on her juicy kat, making her eyes roll to the back of her head, curling her toes every time, only to slide it back in slow and he would repeat this until they came in unison. She wasn't letting him go for anything in the world.

Aleyah was only fifteen at the time they met, she was also still living at home with her parents. They didn't mind that their daughter was dating a seventeen-year-old boy since he seemed to be taking good care of her, which was surprising, considering they were Christians. They allowed Mike to come by to spend time with her whenever he wanted, that way Papa-J could keep a close eye on them. Eventually he allowed Mike to stay over after he caught Mike trying to sneak out of their 2nd floor window. One night Papa-J was out on the porch having a smoke when he heard commotion in the tree. "What the hell!" He yelled. Mike was startled and fell completely out of the tree landing on the ground. At first he was upset, but once Mike hit the ground, he figured that served as a justified punishment and burst into laughter. Letting Mike stay over didn't work well because by the end of the summer Aleyah was pregnant with Autumn.

While Aleyah was pregnant, Mike-Red was busy in the streets searching for a new hustle. He wanted to be prepared for his baby girl so he went to the "old heads" for advice on how to increase his money. They suggested he get his feet wet in the pimp game. It was the perfect new hustle for him - he could sell drugs and pussy to a new clientele. Mike-Red took the idea and ran with it. He rounded up six girls ranging from ages eighteen to twenty four, who had low self-esteem and a high desire to be wanted by a man. The girls loved Mike because he made them feel safe, attractive and loved. He stroked their egos, making them feel special. Those girls would get on boulevard and turn tricks all day and night for Dirty Red. This helped him double his cash flow.

Of course Aleyah didn't have a clue about his new venture. Mike-Red was slick enough to keep this hustle going for three years without her finding out. That is until somebody got sloppy. One of his hoes called his phone in the middle of the night while he was sleeping and Aleyah answered. The hoe was interrogating her, asking questions as if she was his "bottom bitch" instead of his lady.

Aleyah was livid at the thought of her man pimping. Something had to change quickly, so she confronted him with an ultimatum, he was given two options: his family or his hoes. Mike had made more than enough money in that business, so he chose his family. Mike now had the means to move his family into a home of their own. This was right on time because Aleyah was pregnant again with another baby girl. That's when her parents stepped in, sitting Mike and Aleyah down for a grown up conversation. They explained that it was time for them to marry since they had been in a relationship for four years and had one baby and now a second on the way. The young ones agreed and in Aleyah's seventh month of pregnancy, they were married.

Chapter 5
On The Run

Mike and Aleyah had been living on their own for about two years and were happy having personal space of their own. Mike maintained his household and his three girls very well. They didn't want for anything because he always made sure his girls had more than enough.

One evening Aleyah was braiding Autumn's hair for school the next morning when Mike came in with his gambling buddy, June, around 8 pm. They set up for a crap game while Aleyah put Autumn and baby Naomi to bed. She knew the boys were getting ready to gamble and they would get rowdy, talking shit and slapping their hands on the table. Mike-Red was a genius at shooting dice. His long history of being in the streets helped him develop amazing skills. Impressively, he was always a winner. Mike-Red and June had gambled for at least five hours straight, and by 1:30 am Autumn was awakened by her parents rushing and in a panic. "We have to go, hurry put your clothes on!" yelled Aleyah.

"What's wrong mommy?" asked Autumn. "Where are we going?"

"Just come on, we'll explain later."

An uneasy feeling overwhelmed Autumn. Even as a young child she was curious and observant about everything that came in her sight. She could identify tones, body language, and vibes even when she couldn't quite understand the verbalization.

Ten minutes later, they were burning rubber down the highway at 100 mph. Mike and Aleyah were looking over their shoulders. At this point, Autumn was both terrified and confused. She wanted to know what had taken place in such a short period of time for things to go from June hanging out at their house with her dad to them being involved in a high-speed chase. June was following close behind and it didn't make any sense. Mike instructed his girls to hide on the floor of the car.

As they continued driving June pulled up alongside of their car shouting. "Give me back my damn money!" he yelled.
"I'm not giving you back shit! You lost fair and square nigga! You know how the game goes!"

Mike punched the gas and darted in and out of traffic, finally losing June. He dropped the girls off at Aleyah's parent's house and went to hide the car.

Papa-J was waiting at the door with his shotgun ready to take on anything - or anybody in this case. He motioned to Aleyah to let her know it was safe for her to make a move. She jumped out of the car, grabbed her kids and ran into the house while Papa- J stood in the front yard, checking around to make sure the coast was clear. Autumn cried for her daddy as they ran towards Sweet-Ma, who was waiting in the kitchen to guide the girls upstairs. When they got upstairs they dropped to their knees to pray asking the good Lord to protect their family. After they prayed, Sweet-Ma fixed them a bowl of her delightful beef stew. Everyone calmed, when they realized God had heard their calls, because Mike finally came running through the door. Sweet-Ma always knew how to soothe a womb. Autumn always believed that her grandmother could heal the world with her love and prayers.

Early the next morning Mike and Papa-J went out for a few hours. They returned with two duffle bags filled with guns. They had glocks, revolvers and ooze's. Autumn had never seen anything like this aside from her Papa-J's shotgun collection that he used for hunting. She was petrified. Once again, Sweet-ma took baby Naomi and Autumn upstairs to watch "The Fresh Prince of Bel-Air" while the men handled their business.

A few days later the threats began. There would be the sounds of tires screeching around the house late at night and phone calls every minute on the hour. Things got so chaotic that Papa-J forbade the women to leave the house. They were confined to four walls, which meant no sitting outside on the porch, playing in the yard, or going to the store. The men were sleeping in shifts, watching the windows and running all the errands. Mike-Red's gambling habits had caught up with him and begun to threaten the safety of his family. June even left a couple of threatening messages on the answering machine. "I know where your daughter goes to school, give me my money or I will kidnap her and torture the shit out of her. If you don't believe me, just try me."

After a week in hiding Mike went to get some things from the house. When he arrived the door had been kicked in, so he grabbed his gun and carefully tipped in. To his dismay everything had been stolen and the few things that were left were broken or torn apart. June and his crew had delivered Mike a resounding message. They also hoped they would find something of value, and if they were lucky, maybe Mike had stashed some money or product somewhere in the house. Mike-Red was much smarter than that though. He never brought drugs home and he had a special place where he hid his money, a place that only he and Aleyah knew about.

When Mike returned with the news, Papa-J didn't take it too well. He was more than angry - he was outraged! "This story just isn't adding up Mike. This man is threatening your family over a few hundred dollars he lost in a crap game? This just doesn't make any sense to me. How much did you beat him out of?"

"I beat him for $30,000. I won fair and square, so he has to take the L on that one. That money is mine!"

Papa-J's eyes nearly popped out of his head. He was in utter shock. "Damn boy, you sure have a knack for gambling, huh? But on a serious note, son you have to give some of that money back. You're risking the lives of your family over money? This man knows where you rest your head and he will not stop until he gets what he wants. What's more important? Do you want to be watching your back for the rest of your life? Money comes and goes, but family is forever."

Mike had never experienced the guidance of a father figure. His influences were the thugs in the neighborhood. Their mentality was simply to get money at all costs - never considering the consequences. His father-in-law's words of wisdom helped

Mike open his eyes to a few things that day. After their man-to-man conversation they put a plan in motion to turn down the heat and get things back to normal. The conclusion was to arrange a meeting to settle the feud.

Papa-J planned to do all the talking since the young boys were still at each other's throats.

When June arrived, Papa-J greeted him with his largest shotgun and a mouth full. "Young man let me drop a few words on you. You don't know me but here's the real, I will kill anyone who threatens any of my people. I kill for a living and I would love to put a hole in your bitch ass! The only reason I don't have your body hanging in the back shed now is because of my wife and my girls. So, don't ever bring your ass anywhere near my family again. If you were to even breathe their names you won't be around to take another breath! Now, let's get down to business. We're prepared to give back $15,000, which is half of the money you lost. You do understand that in gambling there's a 50/50 chance that you're going to lose? So keep that in mind next time you decide to gamble at such a high stake."

June was petrified, he had heard in the streets about Papa-J's reputation and now he was face to face with the man. June quickly apologized and assured Mike and Papa-J that it would not happen again. After shaking hands Mike handed June the money and it was settled.

Once the feud had been settled between the men, Autumn felt free as a bird. She had missed two weeks of her classes and was ready to get back to school. Despite being so young, Autumn was going through a lot at the time. With her life jeopardized behind ignorance and greed, she was having a hard time processing the situation. It was in that moment that something in her awoke and she was different. She couldn't quite understand her emotions... She had questions and began searching for answers.

Why would your "friend" threaten your family? Why would you bring the streets into your home where your family rests? That was her first lesson of life. She learned from her parent's mistakes, not ever wanting to turn back those pages, this experience helped shape Autumn.

Chapter 6
Night Creepers

Mike decided to purchase a new house with his half of the money. He thought it was best to give his family a fresh start so that they wouldn't have to relive the nightmares every time they walked through the doors. Of course with a new house came more responsibility, therefore, Mike-Red was putting in overtime in the streets to maintain their new lifestyle. He spent most his time doing dirt and neglecting his priorities at home. In his mind, as long as the bills were paid, food was in the fridge and Aleyah could shop, his job was done.

That was true to a certain extent, but he hadn't considered the intricate details. His lady was a young mother responsible for two kids, a house and a wild thug who kept late hours. She soon grew overwhelmed and lonely.

Autumn awoke to the sound of her father leaving for his
4 am taxicab shift. She crawled out of the bed to watch him through the window. She was always sad to see him go because he was hardly ever home and she missed spending time with him. Mike always made Autumn feel like she was the most special girl in the world. After he drove

away, Autumn got back into her bed, curled up with her favorite bear he had given to her and dozed off.

She was awakened when she heard footsteps coming up the stairs. Soon, she heard giggles, followed by noises of ecstasy. A thump on the wall startled her so much that she jumped out of the bed to follow the sounds. To her surprise, she found her mother in the living room straddling her dad's best friend Quincy. "Mommy why is Quincy here? Daddy's at work." Aleyah looked like a deer caught in headlights.

"Autumn what are you doing up at this hour?"

"The loud noises through the wall woke me up."

"Everything's alright your dad sent Quincy over to check on us while he's working. He was helping me move some furniture around, go back to bed."

"Ok, good night," said Autumn as she went back to bed.

As Autumn tried to get back to sleep, she couldn't shake the vision of her mom on top of Quincy's lap or the loud noises she recognized from her parents room. Autumn tossed and turned the rest of the night because she knew deep in her heart that something wasn't right.

The next morning was filled with tension. Autumn barley said a word during breakfast. She wanted to but was confused and afraid to ask questions. Aleyah was fearful that Autumn would mention her little secret to Mike. She knew how close they were. It was true, she was daddy's little princess and never wanted to see him hurt. She had mixed feelings about what she saw, but didn't want to be the cause of her family breaking up, so she kept quiet. They had already been through a lot and Autumn couldn't carry another burden. But she would always remember the betrayal she felt.

Later that day when Mike and Aleyah came to pick Autumn up from school, she noticed blood all over the seats and windows of the car. They both had blood on their faces and hands as well. Tears streamed down Autumn's face as she sat in the back seat listening to her parents exchange harsh and disrespectful words and a few blows towards each other as if she was invisible. At that moment Autumn wished that she was somewhere else. Then she remembered something that she learned in school earlier that week. Her teacher explained how writing down her feelings would be a great way to release the pain. Autumn pulled out her notebook and wrote a poem about kindness. It expressed how she wanted her parents to treat each other.

That night was worse, Mike was so upset that he left the house and didn't return home at all that night. Aleyah stayed up on the phone with her girlfriends talking about where she assumed he was. Her guess wasn't even close.

Mike had spent the night next door with their sexy neighbor Claudia, he had a thing for her since they moved into their house. He figured what better opportunity to get a piece of Claudia's cookie than now. Mike also wanted to get even with Aleyah for screwing his best friend.

The next morning as Aleyah was making breakfast she got a call from a girlfriend who lived across the street. The friend told her that she saw Mike leaving from Claudia's a few minutes ago. Moments later, Mike came in as if nothing had happened. He kissed the kids, got undressed then laid in the bed. As he drifted off to sleep, Aleyah decided to bring him breakfast in bed, she entered the room like a mad woman throwing hot boiling grits all over him. The sound of pain that shrieked from his body made Autumn cringe. "I hope that nut was worth it!" she yelled.

Autumn ran to the room to find her father covered in grits with a hole in his underwear and crying like a baby. She walked closer to see if she could do anything to help, but Aleyah yelled for her to leave the room and go grab the phone.

Mike had to be rushed to the emergency room for 3rd degree burns. When the ambulance and police arrived to take the report they asked how Mike had been burned so badly, he simply replied, "I bumped into the stove while the pot of grits was still cooking."

Mike and Aleyah had a strong relationship and vowed to never snitch on each other no matter what happened, so he lied to protect his lady. Although he discovered her infidelity, in his eyes they were now even on the playing field, because he too had been unfaithful.

After the paramedics wrapped Mike in bandages, they placed him on a gurney and rushed him to the hospital. Aleyah cried as she watched the ambulance drive off with her husband. All the nosy neighbors, including Claudia and her husband, were crowded outside to find out what happened. When Aleyah saw her steam began to rise from her body, but she kept her cool because her kids were home. She also needed to head to the hospital with Mike. She knew good and well that she could deal with Claudia later.

Every weekend; Mike, Aleyah and a few of the neighbors would get together to play a game of spades, drink and talk shit. That particular weekend changed the course of things. Claudia came by with her husband as if nothing happened between her and Mike. Aleyah played it cool, acting like she was unaware that anything had gone down. During the game, Claudia was laughing and talking to Aleyah as if they were the best of friends. Aleyah acted as if she was hardly paying her any attention, but on the inside she was boiling mad. Claudia continued to talk, suddenly she couldn't hold it any longer. Aleyah stood up and flipped over the card table. "Bitch you fucked my husband!"

Everyone's face was stoned. All eyes were on Claudia. Claudia's face turned red immediately.

"What?" Asked Claudia.

"Bitch you heard me! Don't lie because he confessed everything."

Claudia was in shock and looked terrified. "I-I don't know what you're talking about, I have a husband."

"Oh you're going to lie to my face? Be woman enough to be honest with me!" She walked toward Claudia, looking her straight in the eyes. Aleyah didn't as much a blink as she closed the distance on Claudia then suddenly snapped.

Aleyah grabbed Claudia by her hair and dragged her to the front door. They fell outside onto the porch and Aleyah started pounding and scratching Claudia's face. She even pulled out chunks of her hair. "Get this crazy bitch off of me!" yelled Claudia. It took three people to separate them.

"Next time you'll think twice before fucking somebody with that stank pussy!" yelled Aleyah.

Claudia picked herself up off the porch and looked to her husband for sympathy. He was pissed. "You know that you fucked up, right? Go pack your shit and get out of my house, we're getting a divorce!" He threw his wedding band to the ground then walked off. Everyone stood in silence as Claudia's world shattered. Aleyah smiled and went into her house - slamming the door.

Chapter 7
Caught with ya hands in the Cookie Jar

Mike had one more week to recover in the hospital, which gave Aleyah a lot of time to think. She couldn't shake the fact that he had cheated with the bitch next door - right up under her nose! Now she wanted to get even, although she just fucked his best friend, that wasn't enough.

She dropped Autumn and Naomi off at her parent's house and told them that she was going out to play bingo. That indicated she would be back in a few days. Aleyah had some dirt she wanted to do and the kids would only slow her down.

Mike had not heard from Aleyah in a few days and had a gut feeling that something wasn't right. He had himself released from the hospital and headed straight home. The feeling he had was right because Aleyah didn't come home that night or the following night. He knew she was up to no good.

When she finally returned home with the kids, they walked into a disaster. The floor model TV had been busted and the furniture was cut into shreds and turned upside down. There was a note from Mike on the fridge that read:

> *Even when you're not in my sight I see you! Keep breaking my heart and you will soon find yourself in more pain than you can endure.*

Aleyah's heart dropped to her toes. She packed up the girls and went back to her parent's house for a few more days. She knew it would take some time to smooth things out with Mike. As always, Aleyah had the remedy to heal her man's heart.

After a few love making sessions Mike had all but forgotten why he was mad at her in the first place. When Aleyah and the girls returned home there was new furniture in the place of all the things Mike had damaged. They were fools in love all over again.

Mike-Red was big time in the drug game. He was well known around town for having quality and consistent product. He loved being a hustler and enjoyed the thrill of living on the edge while bringing in fast, easy cash. He even loved the smell of new money. Mike had been slick enough for several years to not get caught, but his luck was about to run out. He was at one of his homeboy's trap house gambling and winning racks on top of racks, when the police kicked in the door to raid the place. This was the one time his gift of gab couldn't talk him out of trouble. Because he didn't have a criminal record he was sentenced to only one year in prison. All he could think of was how he had disappointed his girls and the time he would be away from them.

Aleyah was devastated, she tried her best to cope with her husband being away, but after a few months of being lonely, she was back on the dating scene. She started seeing a guy named Maxwell, he was attractive, charming and rich - just the type of man she liked. He drove a banana yellow Cadillac, was well dressed and overall a pretty smooth guy. Her family was quite fond of him, since Maxwell had been a friend of the family for years, and he was taking care of Aleyah, Autumn and Naomi very well. As the months continued on, Aleyah started to fall in love with Maxwell and his wealthy lifestyle. Again, she had everything she wanted at her fingertips, doubling what Mike was providing. Maxwell had her nose wide open with trips all over the country, lavish gifts and more money than she had ever seen. Maxwell was showing her things that she had never seen before and she loved it. The memory of her relationship with Mike was left blowing in the wind.

Mike was paroled from prison for good behavior three months early. He was so excited about getting back home to his family he didn't tell anyone but his older brother about his early release. He couldn't wait to surprise them. Mike went to pick up one his cars and headed to the mall to buy his girls some gifts. He left the mall then went straight over to Aleyah's parent's house to see his girls. When Autumn saw her daddy walk through the door she ran into his arms. She missed him a great deal. A few minutes later Aleyah pulled up to the house with Maxwell. Mike's heart shattered as he looked out of the window. Maxwell had just opened the car door for his wife then kissed her on the lips. Mike was crushed.

Autumn felt his pain, she wished that she could have taken it away, but it was too late. Mike stormed out of the house, rushing towards Aleyah and the man who was kissing his wife. "Who the fuck is this?" yelled Mike.

She had her lips locked so tight with Maxwell's that she didn't see him coming, so he startled her. "M-Mike? What are you doing here?" she asked.

"You look surprised to see me! You're at it again, huh?"

"Maxwell is just a friend bringing me home from work. No need to worry." Mike stood face to face with Maxwell. "Stay the fuck away from my wife pretty nigga! If I see or hear of you near her again, I will lay your ass out, literally!" Maxwell stepped back with his hands slightly in the air and walked towards the car with a smirk on his face. "No disrespect man. I was just giving the lady a ride."

Autumn stood in the window crying. Her family was finally reunited and her parents were fighting already.

Mike snatched Aleyah by the arm and pulled her towards the house. "You must think I'm a mutha-fucking fool Aleyah.

I'm so tired of your hoe-ish ways. I should've known that you wouldn't keep your pussy to yourself while I was away." Aleyah couldn't find any words to dig her way out of this situation, she was caught with her hands in the cookie jar, and all she could do was cry and apologize.

Catching Aleyah in the act with another man drove Mike over the edge. Up until this point, Aleyah had never been caught, Mike had his suspicions and he had heard things but was never confronted with them face to face. He was usually the one who was sloppy with his affairs. Now, he was given a dose of his own medicine and was unable to stomach it all, the heartache was too much to deal with. Mike got in his car and sped off, leaving Aleyah in the yard crying her eyes out. "Mike, I'm sorry baby, he doesn't mean anything to me. I love you!" She yelled at the speeding car.

Chapter 8
Blurred Lines

Mike-Red went back to a familiar place where he could find something to numb his pain. He went to his old block to see his home-boys, everyone was excited to see him out. Low on money, Mike asked for some help. His boys supplied him with a kilo of cocaine. This would definitely get him back in the game. He gave the boys dap and drove off.

Mike went to his mother's house where he could have some privacy. He pulled out the kilo, chopped it down with a razor and began sniffing line after line until he couldn't feel his face or the heartache anymore. This was the introduction to his Cocaine habit. Mike was so gone off the coke that he didn't call or return to see Aleyah and the girls for a month. Aleyah figured that he just needed time to get over her infidelity.

When he finally came home, he was different. Aleyah could see the change in his behavior and attitude. She didn't say anything about it because she was just happy to have him home. Sometimes he would leave for days or weeks at a time before returning and when he would come home, he would be higher than a kite! This would start arguments, which led to breaking up furniture, which would scare Autumn and Naomi.

One night he came home after missing for several weeks, walked in the door without saying a word, grabbed a hammer and busted their TV while Autumn and Naomi were watching "In Living Color". Aleyah lost her cool. "What the hell is wrong with you?"

"You're my problem! I'm tired of you hurting my heart! All I wanted to do was be with you and my girls, but you keep giving away my pussy to these bum ass niggas out here who don't give a fuck about you or my kids!"

"I can't do this anymore!" yelled Aleyah. "I have been faithful since you came home and you've been on that shit! That's right, I know that you're doing coke! That shit is messing with your mind and ruining our family! Get the hell out of here and don't come back!"

Mike hung his head in shame and went into the room to pack his clothes. Autumn came in crying, begging her dad not to leave. He ignored her and walked out the door. That was the end of Mike and Aleyah's nine-year relationship.

Chapter 9
The Handsome Rich Devil

Once they split, Aleyah took on a night shift as a nurse's aide to support her girls. This was her first job so she had to get use to the responsibility. Again, she was feeling overwhelmed. One night during work she ran into Maxwell who brought his Aunt into the hospital with chest pains. They spent the later part of the night catching up over a cup of coffee. Reuniting with him reminded Aleyah of why she first took an interest in Maxwell. He was handsome, charming and extremely generous. After she explained her difficulties with her finances, Maxwell offered to take over the bills if she agreed to keep her job. That was the beginning of their relationship.

With Maxwell covering all the household costs Aleyah wanted to move to a bigger place, so she moved the girls to a new apartment in a different neighborhood. The need for a fresh start away from her "cokehead" husband consumed her.

At the time, Autumn was eight years old and her body was developing at a rapid pace. She had full grown breast, hips and a round butt. She stuck out like a sore thumb at school, the boys were making mannish comments about her breast and the girls didn't like her because she got all the attention. Autumn felt out of place, she hated that her body drew so much attention, it was too much for her to handle. The uneasiness started to affect her school work. Autumn tried talking to her mother about it, but Aleyah was too caught up in her new man to worry about the things that troubled her daughter, her main focus was now on Maxwell. She catered to all his needs, making him feel like the king of the castle. He gladly accepted the role by moving in and taking over.

Maxwell was quite the socialite. He had lots of friends that he loved to entertain. He would throw big parties at the house on the weekends. There would be a house full of people, food and drinks galore. There was always some action going on in their home.

Mike was losing his mind being away from his family. Aleyah had completely cut him off from all contact with her and the girls, so he pretty much lived in the streets. He began hearing rumors about his wife and her new man. Buffalo is a small town, so everyone knew each other, and everyone talked about everybody else's business.

The rumors that were floating around were that Aleyah had left Mike for a rapist; a man who had just been released from prison, out on parole for raping a twelve year old girl.

Mike was confused, hurt and in rage all at the same time. His mind wondered why his wife would leave him to be with a rapist. She couldn't have known about this man's history

He did a few lines of coke then drove over to warn Aleyah.

When he arrived, he jumped out the car, ran up onto the porch and started banging on the door. Aleyah snatched the door open and before she could say a word Mike began speaking. "Did you know the man that you have living in the house with our girls is a rapist?"

"You are just jealous because I have a new man in my life that's rich and takes good care of me!" She snapped.

Mike grew furious. "You need to stop being so blinded by his money and listen to what I'm saying! You are putting our girl's lives in jeopardy; all for the sake of the dollar bill."

Aleyah was not listening. She rolled her eyes at him.

Mike's rage continued to flare as he grabbed Aleyah by her arms and shook her. "You gold digging bitch! If my girls get hurt behind your stupidity, someone will die! Do you understand that bitch! I will kill somebody over my babies!"

Aleyah slapped the shit out of Mike's face. "Get your damn hands off of me! Don't tell me what to do! I know what's best for me and my kids! You just worry about getting your next fix, you cokehead! Now you want to be concerned about your family? Get the fuck out of my face!"

Mike was beyond hurt, he didn't know what to do. His blood was boiling from the rage he was feeling inside. The neighbors heard them arguing and called the police, just as Mike raised his hand to strike

Aleyah, the police were pulling up. They jumped out of their car and immediately handcuffed Mike.

Autumn was in the window the entire time watching another fight between her parents and the police taking her father away. When Aleyah came back into the house Autumn gave her a cold stare. "Why do you keep sending my daddy away? I hate you for breaking up our family!"

"Get your ass in the bed Autumn and stay out of grown folks business!"

Autumn ran into her room slamming the door. She cried herself to sleep, drowning in her tears.

The next day, as Aleyah was getting ready for work she asked Autumn to do some laundry. "I don't know how to do laundry yet."

"I'll teach you." Maxwell yelled out with a smirk on his face.

Autumn had never been alone with Maxwell and a weird feeling came over her, so she declined his offer. "You need to learn, let him teach you. It's time that you had some responsibility in this house anyway!" Aleyah yelled.

As they walked down the stairs to the basement Autumn started to feel nervous.

Every step for her got harder, it was as if she was moving in slow motion. As she began loading the washing machine, Maxwell stood behind her and stared. Suddenly, as she had her back towards him, Maxwell ran his hands across her young body, breathing hard and fast in her ear. He gently caressed her breasts, before whispering. "Shhh, don't make a sound. You're a sexy little girl. I've been waiting to get my hands on you." Then he stuck his hands into her pajama pants, sliding his finger between her vagina lips. "Oooh, I bet your kitten is sweet." Maxwell removed his hand from her pants and began sucking his fingers to taste her juices, still holding her close. "Mmm, just like I thought, I'm going call you 'Sweet Pea' short for sweet pussy."

Autumn stood as still as a statue - terrified. Tears streamed down her face but she didn't say a word as he rubbed his dick across her butt. She was confused about a few things; one, why was Maxwell doing this to her, and two, why was her vagina wet? Autumn couldn't fathom the words to describe the filth and betrayal that she felt at that moment.

Once he was done getting his rocks off, he grabbed Autumn by the neck and whispered in a low but stern voice. "You better not tell anyone about this. Do you understand me? No one, or I will kill your father and whomever else I know you love. This is our little secret understand? You are mine so get used to it baby, because I'm not going anywhere. We are going to have lots of fun together. Now, straighten up your face and let's go back upstairs."

Autumn did exactly what he said. The thought of her father being killed pierced her heart. She wiped her wet face and runny nose, and then headed up the stairs. When they got back upstairs Maxwell walked up to Aleyah and kissed her on the lips with Autumn's kitten juices dripping from his mouth. Autumn didn't even make eye contact with her mother, she walked past them and went to her room where she dropped to her knees and began to pray. "Lord please don't let Maxwell hurt my dad, I'll do whatever he asks me. Just please keep my dad safe. Amen."

Chapter 10
Going Through the Motions

Mike got out of jail a week later on bond. While he was locked up his mind wandered in many different directions. He couldn't shake the vision of Maxwell hurting his little girls. This situation needed to be handled, even if that meant doing it himself.

Mike made a second attempt to get through to Aleyah. Again, it resulted in a huge argument. This time Aleyah called the cops and Mike was behind bars again. Truly, his only crime was trying to protect his children. Being that he was on parole, he was given an automatic one-year sentence. Now he really couldn't keep his girls safe, in jail he fell into a deep depression.

He was furious with Aleyah! He felt as if he didn't know who she was anymore. Aleyah knew what he had been through as a young boy and Mike had expressed how adamant he was about his daughters being around certain people. Mike was very protective of his girls, he would only allow certain family members to babysit or keep them over night. He pondered for a few days on the thought of getting full custody of the girls when he was released from prison. That meant he would have to undergo a narcotics anonymous program first, in order for a judge to consider his request.

Maxwell had a rich elderly aunt that he would pick up every night from work. He began requesting that Autumn take the ride along with him to keep him company. She would politely refuse but Aleyah would step in. "You never like to leave the house anymore. You've been locking yourself in the room lately, you should go get some fresh air."

Aleyah didn't realize that Autumn was declining for a reason. Autumn wondered if her mother recognized the fear in her eyes, or if she just turned a blind eye. What really bothered Autumn was that her mother would allow her to leave the house after 9 p.m. with a man. This left Autumn disappointed and scared shitless as she rode off into the night air with Maxwell to a dark empty zone.

Maxwell started leaving the house exceptionally early to pick up his aunt. This gave him enough time to have his way with Autumn in private without any interruptions.
Maxwell would take her to the corner store and buy all the snacks she wanted. Using this form of manipulation made Autumn

her body. She had no idea what she was feeling or why she felt that way, but one thing was clear Autumn was scared to death. She tried pushing him away but Maxwell tightened his grip then he laughed and said. "You're feisty just like your mother that makes my dick hard." She surrendered, remembering his threat towards her father and sat there with her eyes closed, while he took complete control and advantage of her body.

Chapter 11
When Selling A Dream Becomes A Nightmare —Manipulation at Its Finest

Autumn awoke most mornings with a feeling of emptiness. She often dreamed that she was falling from the Grand Canyon where she had been running away from Maxwell, but once the road came to an end, Autumn would jump into the wind in hopes of her wings spreading so that she could fly away. Unsuccessful, she would fall hundreds of feet to the ground, waking her in cold sweats.

From the lack of rest and stress, Autumn had fallen behind in her school work terribly. She couldn't concentrate because she obsessed with uneasiness about the next time her innocence would be stolen away in the night. Autumn's social skills had even begun to fade. She was afraid to allow anyone to get close to her. Since her body was now fully developed, the attention from men and boys at this point was extremely overwhelming. To them she was a piece of meat waiting to be eaten by the lions. The boys were mannish, grabbing her butt and breasts. Numb and void was the only way to describe how she felt. She kept to herself most times writing in her journal. It was her vacation from the real world.

Maxwell used every opportunity available to satisfy his disgusting urges. He didn't care where they were or who was around; he would always find a private area to feel her body up. Autumn had become his new addiction and he couldn't get enough. Maxwell was getting greedy and wanted a secluded place where he could take his time getting high on his newfound drug. Somewhere no one would bother him, a place where he could really let loose. After doing a little more thinking he thought to himself, Aunt Vera's mansion is the perfect place.

Vera usually threw sleepovers for the younger girls in their family, which also included stepdaughters and friends, two weekends out of the month. Maxwell conjured up the perfect scheme. He could introduce Autumn to the girls and expose her to the glamorous life where Vera would coach the girls on how to dress, apply make-up, walk, cook, and clean, and then reward the girls with shopping sprees. This plan would make Autumn comfortable enough to stay the entire weekend with the days full of entertainment and excitement planned for the kids, but once the sun went down the grown-ups would enjoy some fun of their own.

Sending the girls to bathe where Vera would wash their young bodies personally, educating them on the female body parts and hygiene matters, she even took baths with particular girls.

Afterwards, they'd change into their gowns to watch Disney Movies (The Little Mermaid, Snow White, and Beauty & the Beast) making them sleepy and ready for bed. The blood relatives had their own rooms decorated to their taste in pink, purple, and yellow wall paper equipped with full bedroom sets, Barbie's, clothes, shoes, jewelry, perfumes and make-up.

Autumn dreamed of having a similar room someday. Her room was plain with only a bunk bed and a few stickers on the wall that she had accumulated from school or the cereal box. She immediately fell in love with the idea of lavish weekends at Vera's. She had not realized that she, along with the other girls, were being trained to be submissive and seductive to both Vera and her Maxwell.

Vera and Maxwell set up the guest rooms on the other end of the mansion for the other girls (Step-daughters and friends) to stay. In the middle of the night they would crawl into bed with them while the rest of the house was sound asleep.

Autumn was a night owl. Since the incidents had occurred she developed insomnia. Usually she would be one of the last girls to fall asleep because she didn't have Disney movies at home, so when she had the chance to watch them, full advantage was taken. This was a plus for both Vera and Maxwell. As she was watching a movie, Maxwell walked in the room. "Come here Sweet Pea, you look so pretty. You're wearing my favorite color." He took her hand, guiding her towards one of the guest rooms where he closed the door. Autumn entered the room in awe, it was one of the most beautiful rooms she had ever seen. The walls were gold and cranberry with a pattern that screamed royalty. It had a canopy bed set aligned with sheer merlot curtains, mirrors on the walls and a closet as big as Autumn's bedroom. She admired all that she saw. Her daydream was interrupted by Maxwell's voice. "I see that you're enjoying your time here at Aunt Vera's house. This is just a sample of the things you could have Sweet Pea." He pulled her onto his lap, she resisted but wasn't strong enough to get away. Autumn could feel his penis growing inside his pants, he then moaned in her ear. "You feel that Sweet Pea? You get me so excited."

He squeezed Autumn's breasts and then started pressing his hands down on her thighs to bring their bodies closer so he could grind his penis on her butt.

He grew aggressive within a matter of seconds, panting and moaning deep and loud. "I want to show you something sweetie" He unzipped his pants and pulled out his penis.

"Do you know what this is?"

"Yes, it's your private part."

"It's called a dick. Have you ever seen a dick before?"

"No."

"Touch it Sweet Pea, my dick is happy to see you."

Tears immediately began streaming down her face. "I don't want to." She whined. "Please don't make me do this."

"Don't be afraid, it's okay." She stood frozen. Terrified, she closed her eyes in hopes that he would disappear. "Sweet Pea, you have to trust me, you know that I love you, right? This is why I buy all the new toys and nice clothes for you. I wouldn't tell you anything wrong."

Maxwell took Autumn's hand and placed it on his penis, his hands lay atop of hers as he taught her how to stroke his dick. His manhood grew with excitement right before her innocent eyes. "Do you see how happy you make me Sweet Pea? It feels good in your hands, right? You feel how hard and strong it feels to your touch? Keep doing that baby." Standing to his feet, he placed his hands on Autumn's shoulders pushing her down to her knees. "I want you to taste me Sweet Pea put my dick in your mouth. Pretend as if you're sucking on a chocolate ice cream pop, those are your favorites, right?"

"No, please don't make me do that," Autumn protested.

"That's nasty."

He stared straight in her eyes. "Trust me, I won't hurt you. This makes me happy, don't you like to make daddy happy? Open your mouth."

Maxwell stood in front of Autumn, rubbing his dick on her lips. A second later he jammed it in her mouth placing his hands on the back of her head. She gagged, choked and cried. Autumn could hardly breathe, but it didn't bother Maxwell at all, he was enjoying himself too much. As he fucked her mouth, he was yelling. "That's it Sweet Pea, eat this dick. Mmmm, you are my little freak, we share something special that we can't tell anyone about, they wouldn't understand."

The pleasure Maxwell was feeling was indescribable. As Autumn continued, he began shaking a second later he came in her mouth. He then demanded her to swallow it. After she did, he kissed and licked the left over cum off her lips. After he was done he silently tipped out of the room. Autumn sat on the floor crying, and wiping her face. When he returned to the room he had a brand new pink 10-speed bike, the exact bike Autumn had asked her mother to buy for her upcoming birthday. "See what happens when you're a good girl, you get rewarded. I love you Sweet Pea."

Autumn couldn't distinguish her emotions, feeling hurt and happy was an uneven balance that left her confused. Her mind wandered into a series of random thoughts that led her into a dark place. This is where she lost herself.

Autumn didn't know much about sex, nor had she experienced it, but the sexual nature had begun to take course in her body. Whenever she was in Maxwell's presence her body became submissive to him. She experienced tingles in her vagina and sensations through her nipples at the sight of him. Autumn had no awareness of the changes her body was experiencing. She was ignorant, entering womanhood at such a tender age. One thing she did understand deep within her heart was that something was terribly wrong with the things Maxwell was doing to her.

In another light, she was beginning to believe that Maxwell truly loved her. The desire to be wanted and loved is powerful. Autumn assumed that if she gave into Maxwell's demands he would stay around and love her forever. The same wish she had for her father who had been locked away for several months and had not contacted them at all.

Autumn's life was getting dark and her vision became blurry. She often prayed that someone would take her hand and lead her towards the light. She was fighting a battle that she could not win alone. Again she gave up and surrendered. She repeatedly thought to herself:

'Maybe Maxwell was right? He has to love me. If he didn't, he wouldn't treat me so good, or buy nice things for me. I should like making him happy, even if it hurts me.'

Autumn's mind was so twisted that her body had begun craving Maxwell's touch. At night she would masturbate, mimicking what he had done to her and waiting for him to enter her room. Maxwell was successful in brainwashing Autumn's young mind into believing that his abuse was a form of love. This was something she lacked in several areas of her life. She needed an escape, and since she couldn't leave, she decided to take a mental vacation so she pulled out her journal and began to write down her thoughts.

Mike's one-year sentence was coming to an end. Being locked away gave him nothing but time to think. He often had nightmares of Maxwell having sex with his daughters. Those dreams drove him insane. The fact that he was behind bars and couldn't protect his children made him feel like a failure. It reminded him of his own father. He planned to change things as soon as he was released and immediately began building his plan of execution. He was going to get rid of Maxwell one way or another, no matter the consequence. The thought of a rapist living under the same roof as his children had Mike sick every day. He was so out of it, he spent most of his time lying in his cell staring at the walls, zoned out.

Chapter 12
The Two Faced Joker

Maxwell surprised Aleyah with an all-expense paid trip to Las Vegas with her girlfriends for her birthday weekend. He even offered to take care Naomi and Autumn while she was away. Aleyah gladly accepted then began to pack. As she was packing she was thinking to herself. *That is why I love that man. I won't ever give him up. He's too good to me.* Before she took off into the friendly skies, she put that juicy on him to extend her gratitude for his generous gesture. He went straight to sleep and for a minute he too was flying in the friendly skies.

The next evening Maxwell hosted a spade night. His family and friends including his two children were there. The adults were talking loud and belligerent. They were sipping on Hennessey and coke, and passing joints back and forth while slapping their cards down on the table.

They lived directly across the street from a K-Mart and all the children in the neighborhood would come play in the huge parking lot. This gave them great space for running, riding bikes, and playing games. When Autumn went into the house to grab a cold drink, Maxwell caught a glimpse her. Lust quickly filled his eyes. Autumn could feel him watching her. Not making eye contact with anyone, she hung her head low instantly, falling into a trance because she knew what was coming next.

She kept her cool walking by the table of adults getting wasted. Breathing deep, her heart once again was pounding in her chest, so loud that her eardrums were thumping to the same rhythm. She silently prayed that he would be too occupied with his company to give her any attention. Her hopes soon failed. Maxwell grabbed her by the arm, asking if she could help him refresh the snacks for the guests. Autumn understood the code for: assume the position. With every step she took towards the kitchen, her entire body went numb, even her ears had tapped out, leaving her walking lifeless.

Once they reached the kitchen Maxwell began yelling, "The bathroom is a mess, we have guests over. Do you want them to think that we're dirty people?" That was a cover-up for whom-ever was watching as he pushed her into bathroom. He closed the door quickly and quietly.

Looking Maxwell straight in the eyes, Autumn sarcastically said, "I'm sure if they knew what you're doing to me they would feel that way, anyhow."

You could see the steam blowing out of his ears and without a second thought he backhanded her across the face, and then caught her before her body hit the floor. "Oh you're being disrespectful now, after all that I've done for you? You must think you're grown. I definitely don't have a problem with showing you what grown-ups do!"

Autumn was in shock from being slapped. She couldn't speak trembling with fear, and she held her bloody lip, while she watched Maxwell snort a line of Coke from the side of the tub. Autumn closed her eyes that burned with tears to pray silently. *'Oh lord, please take me away from this bad man. Please bless me so that I never have to see his face ever again. Amen.'*

She wished that when she opened her eyes she would be alone in the bathroom, hell - alone in the entire house! But reality set in when she peeled her lids open. Maxwell was still standing in front of her looking like a drugged version of the incredible hulk. Instead he was the incredible demon. The Coke had taken affect. The rims around his eyes were red with a raw look to them. He had white powder on the borders of his nostrils and on his lips he wore an evil grin. "I told you from the beginning to keep your mouth shut. If you had listened I wouldn't be upset right now. You'll learn a good lesson tonight."

He aggressively grabbed her by the pants ripping them down to her ankles. He then forcefully snatched off her shirt exposing her bare breast.

"Yeah, let me see that beautiful body. You have great tits too be so young, Mmmm, you are nice and ripe!"

Maxwell pushed Autumn onto her knees before shoving his fingers into her vagina, deep and hard. "I see that you're talking back, saying bad words to hurt daddy's feelings. I need to clean out your mouth, open it!"

He thrusted his dick inside her mouth, bloody lip and all. He demanded her to suck on it like her favorite chocolate ice-cream pop, which she had completely lost an appetite for. He placed his hand firmly on the back of her head to make sure that she was taking it as far as it would go into her throat. He threatened that if she gagged she would have to suck his dick all over again. Autumn's jaws were cramping and her lips were throbbing from the slap. Finally the nasty bastard exploded, all in her mouth, demanding her to swallow it. Maxwell didn't see an innocent little girl in front of him, what he saw was his private whore.

Autumn strained to keep her composure she wanted to vomit. She also wanted to bite his dick off and stick it in his mouth. She was tired of being violated. Evil feelings had begun to come over her. She plotted quietly in her mind thinking of ways to poison Maxwell as she swallowed his demon babies.

He walked over to the sink to clean up before heading back out to their guests who hadn't even noticed that they were missing. Before Maxwell left the bathroom he turned to Autumn, "I bet you'll remember to keep quiet, won't you Sweet Pea? Get used to me, I'm here to stay."

Before walking out of the bathroom, he straightened up his shirt and did a final face check in the mirror, "I'm going to ask your mother to marry me, that way you'll be mine forever." Then he walked out of the door.

Autumn sat on the floor hugging her knees rocking back and forth, thinking to herself, *'He wants to marry my mom? What a joke!'* Then the realization of what he said really hit her, *'Oh my God, I know how in love my mom is with Maxwell and his money, this torture will never end!'* It was at that moment she felt trapped within the four walls as she sat crying her eyes out.

Autumn had been going through this well over a year now and Aleyah still hadn't suspected a thing because she was too busy shopping, getting her hair and nails done and traveling to see that her daughter was dying internally right before her eyes. Autumn's thoughts channeled to her father. *'Where is my dad when I need him?'* She stood to her feet and starred at the mirror, she no longer recognized the girl she saw, her eyes were filled with emptiness. She was face to face with a familiar stranger asking. *'Who are you?'* Sadly there was no answer.

One thing was certain; she had mastered wearing a mask to cover the ugliness that consumed her. Autumn washed her face, brushed her teeth, straightened her clothes and went back to join the crowd. Maxwell had her trained to act as if everything was good. She took a deep breath and walked back through the house wearing a smile on her face and a scar on her heart as she refreshed the guest's drinks and snacks.

Chapter 13
An Eye for an Eye - A Tooth for a Tooth

Autumn hadn't had a full nights rest in over a year. Most nights she sat up starring out at the stars in the sky, crying and praying that her dad would come save her from the monster that lived in the house. Her faith wouldn't allow her to give up. She believed to the depths of her soul that God would bring her father back some day.

Mike had finally been released from prison without telling anyone except his mother and brothers. He was ready to implement his plan in taking Maxwell out, but he needed to move in silence so that he didn't get caught before his plan could be put into play. Mike-Red was well connected all over the city, so he had eyes watching Maxwell's family. His plan was to find out where Maxwell's immediate family lived in case he couldn't get directly to him, so that he could torture his family. Mike was ruthless at this point and felt he could get "an eye for an eye" if nothing else. Mike was not going to let anyone get in the way of protecting his children anymore. He started out by following Maxwell's mother and sister, learning their day-to-day routines. That's when Maxwell's brothers started showing up, which was a jackpot for Mike. He knew where the entire family lived and worked. Now it was time to make somebody pay.

Mike rounded up five of his goons. "It's time to send this nigga a message. You fuck with my family and I'm gonna fuck with yours! Let's kick in some doors, rob and torture these mutha-fuckas. They have plenty of loot so everybody will get a nice cut. June and Ray, you'll take his brother, he lives over there on Gennesse street. Keith and Joe, you can take his sister, she's fine so have fun with her! She lives over on Doat rd. Duke and I will take his mom. I have special plans for that bitch. Here are the addresses and blueprints of the houses and where they stash their cash. All right, let's ride or die niggas! He'll never know what hit him."

Before the gangsters rode out they all did a few lines of coke. A few even took a hit of heroine chasing it with bottles of Tanqueray or Whiskey. They strapped up with their nine millimeters and hit the streets. Like clockwork the doors of Maxwell's mother, sister, and brother were all kicked in at the same time.

The gangsters showed no mercy. Maxwell's brother was pistol-whipped, then had a broom shoved up his ass. His sister was beat unconscious and raped. Mike took his time with Maxwell's mother slapping her face until it turned blue. He tied her to a chair leaving her dangling from the second story porch.

The gangsters met back up later that night to share their stories. Mike was impressed with his boys work. They had pulled it off without being seen. Collectively they had over eight thousand dollars. Mike split the money between his boys without taking a cut for himself.

He decided to lay low for a while at his mother's house. He spent the idle time flying through the galaxy, snorting coke lines back to back. This would cloud the visions of what he had done to Maxwell's family. Although Mike had been a gangster for fifteen years, this stunt was by far his worst. He had left their family for dead and now the reality had set in that there would be consequences for his actions. All he could do was wait to see what was coming to him. He didn't eat, sleep or communicate with anyone. He just sat in his favorite chair, mute, starring at a blank television.

...

Autumn awoke with her father on her mind and heart. She decided to call over to her grandmother's house to see if anyone had heard from him. When she called her uncle

Alain answered, excited to hear from her. "Hey Uncle Alain, it's Autumn."

"Hello baby-girl, long time no hear. How are you?"

Autumn burst into tears. "I'm not happy at all, I really miss my dad, have you heard from him?"

"Baby-girl, dry your eyes. I have good news for you. Your daddy is here, he was released a few days ago. He needed some time to get things in order but he's taken care of that. Why don't you all come by, I'm sure that he'll be happy to see you girls."

"Thank you Uncle Alain, I'll see you soon."

Autumn rushed into Aleyah's bedroom to share the news. "Mom, guess what? My dad is home, he's at my grandma's. Can you please drop me off over there? Please."
"When was he released?"
"A few days ago, can we please go see him? I miss him so much."
"Sure, let me grab my shoes."

Autumn was excited the entire car ride to her grandmother's house. Her mind went in a million different directions. She assumed the release of her father would also mean freedom for herself. She just needed to get him alone so that she could tell him what she had been going through. She was confident that once her father knew, he would set her free. She smiled to herself as she anxiously waited to be reunited with her soon to be hero.

When they arrived at her grandma's house, Autumn jumped out of the car and ran to the door, leaving Aleyah and Naomi behind. She began knocking as fast and as loud as she could. Uncle Alain opened the door to a huge hug from Autumn who was obviously happy to see him. Alain told her that her father was upstairs in the den. She ran up the stairs with much excitement. As soon as she saw him tears rolled down her face. She was so relieved to see him.

Autumn jumped right on her dad's lap and hugged him so tightly. "Daddy, I've missed you so much." she whispered in his ear, "I have so much to tell you."

Mike sat there gazing into space as if he were in deep thought. "Daddy, aren't you happy to see us?"

As soon as Aleyah and Naomi walked in the room Aleyah realized that Mike was high out of his mind. "Autumn baby, come on lets go. Your dad isn't feeling well right now, we'll come back another time."

Autumn's tears flowed like a river. "Daddy, why are you ignoring me? Please say something, I need you." He had no interest in seeing his family. He lacked emotion to be precise. After countless attempts to get his attention, she gave up. As they walked out of the room, Mike managed to mumble a few words, "Run, they're coming! I hear them, Hurry up!"

Autumn thought to herself, *'clearly this man has lost his mind.'* but was curious to know who he thought was after him? "Dad, who are you talking about?"

"The FBI!" he blurted out. Suddenly he jumped out of his chair, grabbing both Autumn and Naomi, demanding that they crawl into a hole that was located inside of a wall that he made as a hide-away.

"Get your damn hands off of my kids, you crazy bastard! This is why I don't allow you to see them, because you can't leave that bullshit alone! Thanks for showing your kids how much of a crack-head you really are!"

Aleyah took her children by the hand and lead them out of the house. Autumn was screaming, begging and pleading. She did not want to accept the fact that she had to go back home to a monster. Especially when her father was right in her face. A piece of her heart broke off that day. She had witnessed her dad lose his mind in front of the family. Furthermore, there was no hope for him saving her from the misery that consumed her life.

Back at the house Maxwell received a call stating that his mother, sister and brother had all been rushed to the emergency room. When he arrived and saw the horrible conditions they were in, he realized someone wanted to send him a message. He was unsure however which enemy had almost killed his family. Maxwell broke down in tears.

Chapter 14
Spring Cleaning

Aleyah was working while Maxwell, Naomi and Autumn were at home spring cleaning. Maxwell was still trying to wrap things around his brain, wondering who wanted his family dead and who he needed to watch out for. His temper flared as his mind scanned through all his known enemies. There were too many to come to a complete conclusion. He was so upset that he needed to get even with the world somehow.

Looking out into the living room where the girls were, he watched Autumn as she sat on the couch counting loose change. He had to do something to alter his mood so he sent Naomi to her friend's house a few doors down. When Naomi walked out of the door he locked it, then went to take a hit of his white poison.

Autumn was still sitting on the couch when he walked back in the room, picked her up and carried her as if she was his newlywed bride crossing over the threshold. He carried her into the bedroom that he shared with Aleyah, laying her gently on the bed. He took some cocaine and shoved it up her nose - making sure she inhaled it. He then began to fondle her aggressively while lying on top of her.

Maxwell was breathing hard and deep as he tried to unfasten Autumn's pants. His dick was hard as a rock and she could feel it through his pants. At that point Autumn was high as a kite and losing all her sanity. She started fighting Maxwell and yelling loudly, "Get off of me Maxwell!" Her head was spinning, her stomach was queasy and she couldn't feel her face.

Her screams didn't faze him at all. He was turned on by her feistiness, but her loud mouth was getting out of control so he punched her in the face to quiet her down, blacking her eye and swelling it immediately. That didn't stop her from fighting. Maxwell pinned down her arms with one hand and pulled her pants down with the other, while kissing her neck before hostilely penetrating her young sacred walls. Tears flowed from Autumn's face as she screamed. He however moaned with great satisfaction. His two hundred and fifty pound body was no match for a girl who barely weighed eighty pounds soak and wet. "Don't you love my mother? Please, let me go!" yelled Autumn. Maxwell laughed and whispered in her ear, "Yes, I love your mother. That's why I'm going to marry her, that way I can have the both of you. Now, stop fighting me and give me this sweet pussy, it's so good and tight. Come on relax and take this big dick from your new step daddy."

Every stroke burned. Autumn could feel her walls being ripped apart as they wrestled all over the bed. "I like that you're feisty, it turns me on. It makes me want you even more." Then, he wrapped his hands around her neck choking her and forceful stroking her. With the combination of the pain from her walls being torn, him cutting off her air supply and the coke affect, Autumn fell unconscious. She awoke to Maxwell licking her face. Blood was all over it and her vagina as well. Suddenly Autumn felt the strength of ten men. She began beating him in his chest, which was problematic because Maxwell had asthma. As she fought for her freedom, she managed to strike a mighty blow hard enough to knock wind from him. Maxwell jumped up immediately searching for his asthma pump. Once he jumped up, Autumn ran out the bedroom, out of the house and down the street. She had no specific destination, but she wanted to get as far away from him as imaginable.

As she sprinted down the street half dressed with tears racing down her swollen face questions filled her head, *'Where can I go? Who can I turn to? Who will protect me? Who will believe me? Who can I trust?'*

She was too deep into her thoughts to hear or see that Maxwell was right behind her, shouting out her name. Autumn tried as best she could to get away, but he caught her, swooping her off her feet and bear hugging her. She shrieked, "Get off of me!" as the tears continued to drown her face. He whispered in her ear, "Please don't tell anyone, I'm sorry. I won't do it again."

She was still screaming and crying, "Let me go! Get your hands off of me!"

He carried her back towards the house they called "home", which in her case was more like a dark hole. As they got closer to the house, Autumn's best childhood friend, Nikki, was coming up the street. Autumn was grateful to see a familiar face, but just as she began to make eye contact with Nikki to communicate that something was wrong, Maxwell buried her head in his chest to hide the bruises on her face. He started making jokes with Nikki and just like that, Nikki laughed and continued on with her day.

Once they got back in the house, Autumn sat on the floor in the corner crying. She rocked back and forth as her young mind went in a million different directions. Still trying to come down from the poison she thought to herself, *'this can't possibly get any worse. Is this really my life? Will I seriously have to learn how to accept such a violating nature?'* Autumn's thoughts had run rapid. She couldn't shake the piercing feeling in her body, she eventually blanked out and went into mental shock.

Maxwell went straight for his Cocaine stash and started sniffing a line while choking with it all over his nose and mouth. He shouted, "All I did was love you and your family! I was there for you! I gave you everything you wanted and this is how you repay me?"

Autumn didn't hear a word he said, she was still in a trance. Maxwell began crying and packing his things in large garbage bags. By that time Naomi was at the front door knocking to come in. Autumn quickly snapped out of it, jumped up and unlocked the door. Naomi was confused when she saw Maxwell crying and packing.

Naomi cried out, "What's going on?" Neither one of them answered; so she asked again. "What happened? Max, where are you going?"

"I love you girls so much, but I have to leave".

Joy filled Autumn's heart when she saw him grabbing his belongings. But now, the million dollar question that kept swarming around her brain was, *'How am I going to explain this to my mother? She will never believe me. I will be the one blamed for him leaving.'*

Her excitement quickly dissolved. As Maxwell walked toward the door he hugged the girls, gave them money to buy candy and then he left them all alone.

After he was gone Autumn took a shower to wash away the dirtiness of Maxwell. Then she walked Naomi to the candy store. Overlooking the crazy events of the day, she went back to relishing her childhood once again.

Chapter 15
When the Shit Hit the Fan

Autumn and Naomi were sitting on the porch when Aleyah and her sister, Nina, pulled up in front of their house. Their aunt called both girls over to get inside. When the doors opened Aleyah was crying her eyes out, yelling, "What happened to your face?"

Autumn hung her head, afraid to tell her mother what Maxwell had done. She could only utter a single word, "Max…"

"He did this to your face? Why didn't you tell me that he was hurting you?"

Instantly overwhelmed, Autumn began to cry.

"I was afraid! He told me not to tell anyone or he would kill my father!"

Aleyah and Autumn cried in unison while everyone else was silent, awkwardness rising amongst them.

After Maxwell left the house he went to see Aleyah at work, confessing to the raping of her daughter. When he told her what he had done she lost it. She picked up a chair nearby and threw it at his head. After that Aleyah called her sister Nina. Nina called 911 to file a report because Aleyah was too distraught to have a conversation with anyone. When the police arrived, the severity of this situation finally hit Autumn like a ton of bricks. The policeman, Officer

Sheppard, asked a series of questions, wanting full details. "Autumn can you tell us what Maxwell has been doing to you? Don't leave anything out."

She was embarrassed as she searched for the appropriate words to explain the dirty details of her abuse. "Maxwell would sniff that white stuff then he would put his penis in my mouth and make me suck it." Autumn felt naked and vulnerable as devastated Aleyah and Nina both listened to her speak. "He would beat me." She took a deep breath. "Squeeze my chest and stick his fingers in my private."

Each word that rolled off her tongue spoke of shame and the officers could read the pain on her face. Officer Sheppard looked Autumn straight into the eyes and said, "It's ok, just take your time. I understand that this is hard for you. None of this was your fault. You are just an innocent child. He's a sick man. How many times has he done this to you?"

"I'm not sure, but I know that it's been happening every week since I was eight years old. I am ten now."

"We're almost done. Can you tell us what happened today?" He asked.

At this point Autumn was exhausted and unsure of everything - nothing made sense. She didn't know who to trust or the difference between sincerity and being taken advantage of. She questioned whether or not she could trust the police because they were male- or any other male for that matter. once they left, the phone started ringing off the hook. Everybody was aware of Autumn's dirty secret, which further humiliated her. Aleyah was on the phone trying to explain to her family what happened. As she continued talking there was a loud knock on the door. The people on the outside were calling both Aleyah and Autumn's names. Terrified and regretting her decision to speak with the police, Autumn knew from that point on her life would be complicated.

The knocks at the door went on for hours on end. It was Maxwell's family trying to get the full story. Autumn didn't understand why they would show their faces after all that had happened, especially since they knew that Maxwell was a child molester. *What a disgrace this should be to them.* She thought.

Autumn had no idea how dramatically her life would change over the course of the next few years.

There were countless court dates, speaking in front of The Jury and telling her story about how she had been violated by someone that was a father figure. Explaining how her childhood had been taken away, Autumn felt several different emotions at once - devastation, confusion, filth, and a sense of unworthiness. She had no place where she could rest or feel at ease. Still, non-trusting of anyone who crossed her path, Autumn began to shut down.

Aleyah signed Autumn up for group counseling shortly after the court dates began, thinking that therapy would help her daughter get back to normal. The sessions were extreme, involving several young girls who had been stripped of their innocence as well. This experience taught Autumn that there were more perverts that existed in this crooked cruel world than one could imagine. Listening to the girls share details of how they had been abused in some of the wickedest ways imaginable was gut wrenching.

These stories were disturbing. Some, sexually abused by family members (their fathers, brothers, and uncles) taking part in tarnishing their souls. Autumn was traumatized and after a few sessions she decided she didn't want to go counseling anymore. The exposure to the stories sent her into a state of depression. She couldn't fathom the meaning of love, loyalty or trust. Again, she was lost in the dark, not understanding the difference between reality and deception.

She had no one to turn to. Her family thought the best way for everyone to deal with her abuse was to not speak about it, in hopes that it would magically disappear. She searched for the logic behind the emotions she felt without a shoulder of comfort. All the while, she was trying to find her way back to normality. There was nothing left to do but get on her knees and pray to GOD. She spent many restless nights writing in her journal, lost deep in her thoughts.

Overcoming was a challenge. Her mother was preoccupied chasing M&M, translation, "Men & Money." while her father was strung out in the streets. She locked up her pain in a keepsake box and buried it. Still a child, she didn't know of any other way to cope with it except for blocking it out of her mind.

Chapter 16
Summer Heat - Burning It Down

Several weeks after the shit hit the fan Aleyah had a new friend. His name was Denzel. He was a "big shot" from California. Aleyah sold the story that he was a Psychologist that came to help Autumn deal with her depression. Bullshit! Weeks had passed and Denzel hadn't held any psychotherapy sessions with Autumn. Aleyah and Denzel were so wrapped up in one another that Autumn's issues were not a priority. That wasn't the worst of her problems, Denzel was now living in the house with them and it had only been 8 weeks since Maxwell left.

Autumn's head began to spin as she sat on the bed crying while watching Denzel move his things into their home. She was wondering, *'Will I relive the same nightmare with this man? Will he hurt me the same way or worse?'* She did not trust anyone, especially men. Autumn was very uncomfortable around any man that she came in contact with, and that also included family members, as she vividly remembered some of the stories she heard during group therapy. She died a little on the inside because she could not understand why Aleyah didn't love her and Naomi enough to keep their best interest at heart, instead of her own selfish needs.

Denzel was exceedingly arrogant. He walked around as if he was a king and everyone else was beneath him. Aleyah and Naomi were crazy about him, but Autumn however, kept her distance. The energy around him was negative. Denzel disliked that he couldn't wrap Autumn around his finger as he did Aleyah and Naomi. Trust had become a foreigner to Autumn. Completely disregarding what she had been through and understanding she had every right to be guarded, Denzel decided to complicate things for Autumn. He wanted to show her who was boss.

Although Autumn wasn't very fond of him, she did treat Denzel with respect. He however, treated her completely the opposite. He loved playing the favoritism game with the girls. There were many times when he would go shopping to buy new and exciting things for himself, Aleyah and Naomi, but leave Autumn out. There were even times when he would order take out then he, Aleyah, and Naomi would go into the bedroom to eat, shutting the door behind them. As he closed the door Autumn would ask, "What am I supposed to eat?"

Denzel would snicker, "Don't know, don't care! Do you think when O.J. asks for a glass of water or a hot meal, he gets it? No! Prisoners don't have rights! You only get what I allow you to have. I'm the Warden and you're the prisoner."

Aleyah didn't say a word, she didn't even check to see if Autumn had eaten dinner for the evening. At only eleven years of age at the time, and not allowed to cook anything on her own, she would just go hungry. At this point, Autumn began to feel neglected. She began to quietly wonder if it was something she did to make everyone treat her badly. As she lay across her bed that night, she questioned her character. She asked GOD, *'What is it about me that make others unhappy?*

Please help me change my ways, for I want to be loved too.'

Chapter 17
The Family That Preys

Aleyah, the girls and Denzel moved into a new neighborhood. Denzel and Autumn's relationship soon began to change for the good. It turned out that Denzel had some good in him after all. He was there to support Autumn during her biggest court date. It was the first time she had to come face to face with Maxwell since he raped her. This was one of the worst days of her life. She was afraid to step in front of Maxwell, his family, the judge and the members of the jury. Autumn felt naked again as she aired her dirty laundry about Max in detail.

The pressure made her very uncomfortable, but Denzel was there, so she felt a sense protection for a change. Although she wished that her father would've been there, again, he was missing in action for one of the most important days of her life. She hoped to gain closure by putting away the man who had tainted her forever.

During the trial, Autumn learned that Maxwell was caught raping his ex-wife's niece a few days prior to their court date, which made her feel even worse than she had before entering the courtroom. But, some of her feelings ceased as the jury found Maxwell guilty and sentenced him to eight hard years of prison time. Autumn felt as if she could finally move forward with her life. She took a deep breath and cried tears of joy as she walked out of the courthouse.

Although Maxwell was locked up Autumn was still going through a rough patch. There was a lot going on in her life. Trying to adapt to her new school, making new friends and trying to move forward was overwhelming. Granted, she was surrounded by a lot of new faces, but Autumn still felt lonely. She wondered if people saw her bright personality and warm spirit or did they just see her well-developed body. She asked herself, *'Will I have to sacrifice my integrity again to be welcomed into this new environment?'*

She soon made a friend who seemed as if she was sent from heaven. Her name was Brandi.

Brandi and Autumn had a lot in common so they clicked instantly. They found comfort in each other because they shared two things, both were fully developed and both knew what it was like to be used as a sexual object.

Brandi's story, however, was a bit more raw and uncut than Autumn's. She had a huge family, all of which didn't consist of real family members but people who were extremely close in a twisted type of way.

They created their own definition of family.

Brandi lived next door with her mom Jackie. Her father, David, lived a few houses away with his wife and older son. David's brother Dayle owned several houses on that block, so their entire family lived on the same street.

Dayle owned a trap house across from his brother David and all the teenage boys hung out over there. Autumn, now a pre-teen and boy crazy, was eager to get a piece of the action, but her mother wouldn't allow her to visit that end of the block because she was all too familiar with the lifestyle and she didn't want Autumn involved in any more drama. Brandi's father and uncles were big time drug dealers that were well known around the city as "The Jones Brothers". They had access to everything and anyone money could buy. As the saying goes "cash rules everything around me" and whoever came up with that must've had them in mind.

Autumn lived vicariously through Brandi who was the same age as her, only 12 years old, but much more experienced. When the girls had sleepovers at Brandi's, she would share her world with Autumn detail by detail. The first time she opened up she explained to Autumn that her family lived a different lifestyle than most. Autumn assured her trust and confidence without passing judgment. Brandi went on telling Autumn about how she had been involved in what you call a ménage trios. The term was new to Autumn's ears, but she was excited to learn more about it.

"It was Travis, Marcel and I," said Brandi. "We got drunk and smoked a few blunts and then Travis started kissing me and took my clothes off. I got on all fours "doggy-style" Marcel stood in front of me, I sucked his dick and Travis hit it from the back. Then we switched positions. I sat on Marcel's lap, he put his dick in my ass. Travis kneeled in front of me, I spread my legs across each arm of the chair and he stuck his dick inside my pussy. It was so nasty, but so good!"

Autumn was stunned, but intrigued. It was like listening to live porn. She definitely wanted to know more. "Wow Brandi! Did it hurt? Having two dicks in you at once, I've heard about regular intercourse, but taking it in the ass is on a whole new level. What does that feel like?"

"Well, the first few times it's going to hurt and you may shit a little." The girls giggled in unison. "But once you get used to it, it feels great. I can cum while having anal sex."

"What's cum?" asked Autumn.

"Girl you really are a virgin aren't you?" laughed Brandi. "Cumming is something that happens at the end of sex. It can also be called an orgasm, which is when your body starts to tingle all over and your clit experiences an amazing sensation and then your pussy explodes with a white sticky substance. Afterwards you'll be ready to fall straight to sleep."

Again, the girls burst out with laughter. "Damn, that sounds like fun," said Autumn. "You are a brave one I'm too scary to go all the way with a guy. The thought of his dick ripping open my walls scares me. But, I will continue to take notes for when I am ready, that way I can be a pro like you." The girls high fived and went off to bed.

After that night Brandi and Autumn were inseparable and hung out every day. Listening to Brandi's sexual adventures was highly entertaining and intriguing to Autumn. She visualized the stories and partners as if she was there herself. She wanted a peek into Brandi's world, so against her mother's wishes, she snuck down the street to meet the family.

Brandi's family consisted of overly aggressive men, teenage boys and young girls. The men were in the dope game and ran a few trap houses on the same block where they lived. There was constant traffic in and out of these houses so business was good. They were managed by teenage boys, whose idea of success was selling dope. Autumn had been introduced to a few of them.

Autumn was a fresh fish in their world and Brandi's father, uncles and their crew had a thing for her. The lust in their eyes was evident when she walked into their presence. They whistled and shouted lewd comments without any care. They all hoped to be wearing her on their arm, and she enjoyed the attention, it gave her confidence.

Autumn and Jorden, who was seventeen, locked eyes immediately. He walked over and kissed her hand as he introduced himself. She blushed and continued to stare into his eyes. Their energy was magnetic upon introduction. There was something about Jorden that made him stand out from his crew. He was handsome, charming, and had the swagger of a rough neck, but at the sight of Autumn the rough neck quickly turned into a gentleman. Jorden had already made up in his mind just like his crew that he wanted to make Autumn his lady.

After a few minutes of being in Brandi's world, Autumn began to get nervous. She wondered if her mother had noticed that she was not at Brandi's house, so Autumn said her goodbyes and headed back down the street. Once she was gone the guys made a huge uproar about Autumn, asking Brandi question after question trying to get the scoop on the twelve year old with an angelic face and a body like a coke bottle. They nicknamed her "Coke-Cola". They even made a bet on who would get her first. Jorden didn't participate in the bet, but he had plans of his own.

Since Autumn wasn't allowed to hang out on that end of the block, Jorden had to come up with a plan to communicate with her. Since the day they met, Jorden began to have dreams about Autumn, he even found himself day-dreaming about her slanted eyes and angelic smile. He was determined to be with her, so he found a way to get her attention. He began sending notes attached with a single rose to Autumn and would always pay Brandi to deliver them. The first note read:

You are as beautiful and delicate as this rose! To me you are the prettiest flower that I've laid eyes on. I just wanted to let you know that I can't stop thinking about you. You're always on my mind…In my dreams…

Peace,

Jorden

Autumn was smiling ear to ear with butterflies as she smelled the single red rose Jorden sent. At that moment she experienced her first major crush. Jorden knew just what to say to capture her attention. She laid back on the porch, daydreaming in the sky about Jorden's arms holding her close. She then went in the house and grabbed a sheet of paper and a pen and wrote:

Dear Jorden,
Thank you for the rose and the sweet words, I've been thinking of you too, but my mother is very strict about me having

boyfriends, she thinks that I'm too young. So I'm not sure how we can pull this off, but I'm down to give it a try. Give me a few days to come up with something...

XOXO,
Autumn

Both lovebirds pondered over an idea to see each other on the "low" without her mother finding out. Jorden replied with two roses and cologne scented on the letter:

Autumn,
Whatever I need to do to be with you, I will. I've never met a girl like you. There's something special about you and I wanna

find out what it is. I'll wait as long as it takes because I feel you're worth it. I'll think of something. In the meantime, we can keep in touch through letters and when you can, call me and we'll talk. *893-0428*

Love,
Your new man - Jorden

Autumn had the biggest smile on her face. Jorden had her feelings all wrapped up and she didn't want to be untangled. After weeks of writing letters she couldn't take it anymore, Autumn and Brandi came up with a master plan. Brandi would ask her mom if Jorden could come over to hang out at their home. Jackie allowed Brandi to date, so they figured it was worth a try.

Chapter 18
The Snakes in her background

Jackie agreed to allow Jorden to visit Autumn under the conditions that there would be no sexual contact between them. Autumn agreed to be on her best behavior. She was super excited to relay the good news to Jorden, who was ecstatic as well. They planned to see each other that evening so Jorden decided it would be best if he came in through the back door so no one would see him entering the house. Once he opened the door and saw Autumn's face he picked her up off her feet with a warm hug and kissed her passionately. He stroked her hair, and outlined her face with his fingers while staring deep into her eyes. They talked and cuddled the entire night. "I'm so happy to have the opportunity to spend this one on one time with you," he told her. "You have such a warm spirit and personality. And it doesn't hurt that you are gorgeous."

They both giggled. Autumn blushed until her cheeks were rosy red. She was looking deep in his eyes and told him, "I'm happy to be spending time with you too. I have to be honest, I really didn't expect for you to be so sweet and genuine. Most guys that try to holler at me are into me because of my body and they act as if they like me but they really just want to get my cookies."

"Well, I can honestly say that your body is sexy as hell. When I first saw you all I could think of was 'Damn she's fine from head to toe' Although you are fine, I am more interested in your mind, your heart, and your spirit. Those are the things that will keep my interest. And based on this conversation alone I can see that you are intelligent and mature beyond your year's, that alone is attractive. I must say that I am highly intrigued. You have my full attention baby."

Autumn smiled from ear to ear, she had never had anyone say such wonderful things about her. She was so used to the people putting her down, especially

Denzel. Jorden had no idea how he made such an impact on Autumn's self-esteem. His words filled the empty void that she longed to have filled over the years. At that moment she did something she hadn't in a longtime, Autumn regained trust in a man, her new man Jorden. "You make me feel so safe and beautiful Jorden. I have been through a lot with bad men in my life these last few years and one day I will share those things with you, but I feel protected with you. Something I haven't felt around a man in a very long time."

Jorden could see the pain in her eyes so he held her tighter and kissed her gently on the forehead.

"As long as I am around, you don't have to ever worry about anybody hurting you. I will kick a nigga's ass for fucking with you. That's my word!"

She felt his sincerity within her soul. His words warmed her entire body and made her heart skip a beat. She couldn't hold back any longer and kissed his lips with passion, sucking the bottom lip, then the top and gently sliding her tongue in his mouth, tasting his tongue. She could feel his manhood growing under her. She felt something else too, their hearts beating as one. It was official, they were in love. After a few more kisses, he decided to leave. He was in fact the perfect gentleman.

That night Autumn slept with a smile on her face and joy in her heart. She hadn't been this happy in a while and it felt damn good.

…

Autumn and Jorden met at Brandi's every night for several weeks in a row, they couldn't get enough of each other. His boys grew suspicious, inquiring about his whereabouts after weeks of him disappearing during the night. He finally told his best friend Jaylen about his relationship with Autumn. Jaylen was hyped and couldn't keep this juicy secret to himself. He told another one of their friends Travis, then the word spread like wild fire. Within the next few days everyone on that end of the block knew and that's when things got complicated. There was heat coming from everyone. The guys were jealous because Jorden pulled Autumn and the girls were upset because they couldn't believe Jorden chose Autumn over them.

All of Brandi's uncles were trying hard to reel Autumn in even though they knew she was dating Jorden. Brandi's uncle Dayle was the most persistent. He wanted

Autumn so bad that he propositioned her with a paid allowance and gifts in exchange for her time. She turned him down for several reasons; first, she knew that he wanted to sleep with her, and secondly, she was in love with Jorden. Plus, she wasn't interested in a man who was old enough to be her father, not to mention a drug lord.

Dayle had all of Brandi's friends getting loose, he would host parties, supplying drugs and alcohol and they would have wild orgies. There would only be two or three under-aged girls and five men at the least. One of the girls was Brandi, her uncle would pay them to keep his employees sexually satisfied. Autumn didn't want to be a part of that circle, so she didn't hang out with them.

Autumn soon learned that by the time Brandi was thirteen she had been involved in so many sexual encounters that she couldn't keep up with them all. That's not the worst part about it - Autumn was curious to know where her wild streaks sprouted from, so she asked the million-dollar question and the response she received was more than she had bargained for. "My dad," answered Brandi.

Autumn was confused, she had met Brandi's father and he seemed to simply adore his children. "What do you mean your dad? I don't quite understand."

"Daddy just wanted to make sure that I hadn't been sexually active with anyone so he had sex with me to be sure. That's how he would check."

Autumn sat there in disgust, not saying a word.

"He would make me have sex with my uncle's and his employees, while he watched."

Autumns' mind ran rapid as she thought to herself, *'How sick is that? Making your child perform sex acts, while you watch?'* She became nauseous and petrified. She thought about all the times that she had snuck down the street to hang out at his home. She had no idea she was amongst a rapist, one that preys on his own children. Autumn didn't know what to say. She wished that she hadn't asked Brandi the million-dollar question. Brandi could tell that Autumn was uncomfortable, so she asked her to keep the dirty little secret between them. "Of course, your secret is safe with me. Whatever you and I discuss will always be between us, I've got your back."

The girls embraced each other with a hug then went to bed. Autumn couldn't sleep thinking about Brandi's father and uncles raping her. What made matters worse is that Brandi was completely brainwashed.

She didn't see any harm in what they were doing to her. At that point, Autumn's trust in any man was whole-heartedly gone again. She quietly cried herself to sleep, not wanting Brandi to know that her secrets ate away her heart.

Chapter 19
The Man with Many Faces

Things were going well between Denzel and Autumn, he seemed to be building a bond with her. He even spent time teaching her and Naomi how to cook. He showed the girls how to make mouthwatering lamb chops and cheesecake from scratch. Autumn began to get more comfortable with him around, but she still kept her guard up. She knew that the asshole in him would creep back out at some point. Denzel had many different faces and when he and Aleyah weren't seeing eye to eye, he would get along great with Autumn.

Once they made up however, he would detest Autumn all over again.

Denzel shunned her for having so much love for her father. Because of his addiction, Mike was always in and out of their lives. It didn't matter to Autumn though, she still loved her dad despite his issues, she was daddy's little girl and nothing could change that.

…

Mike attempted to clean himself up by entering a Narcotics Anonymous program. The program required all participants to reside in a halfway house where recovering drug addicts would live under one roof and attend Narcotics Anonymous meetings held in the house - a support group that encourages all addicts to kick their drug habit, stay clean and get a job.

After being in the program for several months Mike went to visit his daughters. They hadn't seen him in two years.
He took his girls to the Marina downtown to hang out by the water, that was Autumn's favorite place, the water gave her peace. Once they got back home Naomi and Autumn rushed into the house to tell Aleyah how much fun they had. Denzel was bubbling with envy as he listened from another room. After listening a little more he came into the living room yelling,

"Ya'll are so happy when your crackhead daddy comes around every now and then! Where is he when I'm paying the bills that you run up? Where is he when I'm putting food in your bellies? Where is he now? Probably out getting high! You two are never this excited when I come into the house. I take care of you, not him!"

"He is our father and I appreciate any time he gives us," replied Autumn.

"Oh yeah? Well you can take your ungrateful ass and go live with him! Oh, I forgot, he doesn't have a home to live in. Well you can go live with him and all his addict friends," said Denzel before bursting into evil laughter. "Yeah, I think that would be best for all of us if you left. So, get your things and get the fuck out! His yelling carried on for what seemed like forever.

Later that evening Autumn was in tears as she went into the kitchen where Aleyah, Denzel and Naomi sat. As she walked toward the kitchen sink Denzel stuck his foot out to trip her. Luckily Autumn had good balance because she was seconds away from busting her head on the porcelain sink top. She was outraged as Aleyah sat a few steps away, watching Denzel without saying a word. It was then that Autumn realized how alone she was in the world. Her own mother didn't come to her defense in fear of losing her man.

Autumn's eyes shot over towards Aleyah with a cold stare, expressing the hurt she felt for her lack of protection once again.

She continued toward the sink, snatching a few plastic grocery bags from the drawer to place her clothes in. She had to leave the house, those were strict orders from Denzel and Aleyah didn't step in to take charge. She left the kitchen and headed toward the back bedroom where her clothes were. Denzel followed close behind, laughing and making fun of her like a child. Once he realized that his childish behavior had no effect on Autumn, he decided to turn up the heat a little, "You ain't nothing but a fast ass little whore! That's right, get your shit and get out!"

Tears poured down her face while her mind raced a mile a minute. She had no idea what her next move would be because she didn't have a way to reach out to her father but she grabbed any piece of clothing she could find and stuffed them into the plastic bags. Denzel continued tearing her down and she tried to ignore him as best as she could, but his words cut like a knife. That's when he lost his cool and grabbed Autumn by the neck, smashing her face into the clothes that lay on the closet floor, giving her no air to breathe. He gripped her throat tighter and tighter as if he wanted her to take her last breath. Gasping for air, she tried yelling for him to loosen his grip, but the words wouldn't come out. Then she tried to get up from the position he had her in. She began tussling with him until he finally decided to release her neck at the sound of Naomi's cry, "Let my sister go, you're hurting her!"

When Autumn turned over to gain her composure, Aleyah was standing there and once again, remained quiet. "You stood there and watched this man choke me half to death?" Autumn asked her mother. Aleyah just stared at her daughter with no compassion in her eyes. Autumn ran into her bedroom, crawled into bed and cried.

She was restless the entire night, tossing and turning while plotting ways to run away. She thought, *'If I had access to a phone I could call my dad to come pick me up, but Denzel made it clear not to touch the house phone. Plus, I have no car or any money, so I'm stuck inside of my own misery.'*

Her mind shifted into a dark place, *'I wonder if I slit my wrists, would it be best for everyone's happiness. Could this be the answer to everyone's troubles, if I no longer existed? That way, I wouldn't have to deal with the struggle of being Autumn anymore.'*

That night she dreamed that she was an eagle who spread her wings and flew to heaven.

The next few days were tough. Autumn quit fighting and became silent. She didn't say a word to her mother or Denzel. She spent most of her time in her bedroom writing letters to Jorden and in her journal, jotting down the dates and times of everything that had taken place between her, Aleyah and Denzel.

...

Jorden was excited when he received a letter from Autumn, he hadn't heard from her in a few days and was worried that something was wrong. Once he read the letter he was furious, he didn't like that Denzel was mistreating his lady and he was going to make sure that it didn't happen again. Jorden was a thug, but was very gentle with Autumn and he damn sure wasn't going to allow anyone to hurt her. He made Autumn a promise to protect her and he was going to make sure he honored it.

He patiently watched and waited for Denzel to leave the house. Denzel was on his way to the corner store when Jorden jumped into his car and followed him. As he hopped out of his car to go into the store, Jorden ran up and punched him in the mouth. That blow knocked Denzel to the ground and Jorden began kicking him in the ribs until blood spewed from his mouth. It took two of his boys to get him off of Denzel. Jorden spat in his face and shouted, "Next time you'll think twice before bullying little girls, won't you? Punk-ass muthafucka!"

The young thugs jumped in their car and pulled off after they heard police sirens. Denzel picked himself up off the ground and headed back to the house. When

Aleyah saw him walk through the door she panicked, "Baby, what happened to you?"

"I got jumped by some ghetto ass niggas at the store."

"Did you get robbed?" she asked.

"No, they didn't take anything. But one of them screamed out something about bullying a little girl."

"That's strange I wonder what that was about."

"Me too."

Autumn heard all the commotion and came out of her bedroom to see what was going on. When she heard Denzel and Aleyah talking, she knew that Jorden had kept his word about protecting her. She went back into her room, closed the door and laughed until it hurt. She smiled as she realized that she finally had someone in her corner, someone who would keep her safe. The love that was growing for Jorden shot to the roof at that very moment. She couldn't wait until she saw him again, her lips ached to be pressed against his and her body craved his arms to be wrapped around her.

The tables turned with Aleyah and Denzel. They were constantly fighting, verbally and physically because he was curious about why he had been jumped by those thugs. In the midst of all the madness Aleyah learned that she was pregnant. Denzel wasn't happy with the news. Even though he had no children of his own, starting a family with Aleyah was not in his plans. He ended their relationship and moved back to California. Just like that, he left her alone and pregnant. She already had a full plate with raising two children on her own, and now she was pregnant again while the father of her unborn child was all the way across the country. Faced with the harsh reality that Denzel was gone and had no intentions on returning, depression soon set in.

Autumn was relieved when she realized that Denzel was gone for good. She felt free as a bird and slept like a newborn. And with her mother in depression mode, she was free to go outside to see Jorden. She also got to hang out with the friends she hadn't seen in a while because Denzel had a habit of keeping her locked in the house.

Jorden was so excited when he saw his lady walking towards him. She greeted him with a huge smile and jumped in his arms.
"Thank you for handling Denzel for me, you really kicked his ass."
"You're welcome baby doll. I can't have anybody fucking with my lady!"
"Yeah, he was so upset that he moved out."
"Word up? Good, that way you don't have to be bothered by him anymore."

"Yes, you have no idea how happy I was to see him walking out the door."

They laughed in unison, kissing and hugging.

...

Mike had begun coming around after being clean for six months. He wanted to make up for the time he lost with his girls. Aleyah didn't object because she longed for the attention of a man after Denzel walked out on her. After a few weeks of Mike being around, she became very comfortable with having him there and asked him to stay the night.

The evening was peaceful as the family slept all in the same house. It had been years since they were all together under the same roof. Autumn's sleep was disturbed by a horrific sound at 4 a.m. She followed the sounds that were coming from the living room where Aleyah lay on the couch. She found her mother sitting up with a pink sack hanging from her vagina. Not knowing what to do Autumn completely panicked.

Her father ran from the back bedroom, also in a panic, "What's wrong?" he asked. Mike had no idea that Aleyah was pregnant.

"I think mom's having the baby!" yelled Autumn.

"Baby? What baby?" asked Mike.

The three of them sat with perplexed looks on their faces. Mike knew it had to be Denzel's child. Autumn could see the pain in his eyes. After sitting there for a moment more he snapped out of his daze and called the ambulance. By the time the ambulance reached the house, Aleyah's sack had burst all over the floor.

When they arrived at the hospital it was too late, she had lost her baby. The stress and depression from the break up caused her to miscarry. Although Autumn hated Denzel, the thought of having a new baby in the house was exciting, but now the baby was gone. That night she had a nightmare about her deceased baby sister's little purple body. She could see the hands, feet, arms, legs, mouth, and eyes. The thought of her lifeless body lying there devastated Autumn.

Mike came back home with the girls and Aleyah, but he was heartbroken. Although he and Aleyah hadn't been in a relationship for several years, he still loved her more than anything in the world. The thought of her having a child with another man struck a nerve. He didn't sleep at all that night and left early the next morning. He was so hurt that he left their house and went to get something that could numb the feeling. After being clean for more than six months, Mike relapsed.

Aleyah hesitated calling Denzel to give him the news, in fear that he would be happy that she miscarried. To her surprise, he was compassionate and invited her to visit him in California for a getaway to help soothe her pain. Aleyah was excited and immediately began making preparations for someone to watch the girls while she was away. She asked her best friend Karrie to watch Naomi and Autumn. The girls were livid because Karrie was very strict, almost worse than Denzel. Autumn made it work to her advantage however. She and Jorden got a chance to spend a few nights together at Brandi's house. Jorden remained a gentleman as he held Autumn and whispered sweet things in her ear each night. Karrie didn't have a clue and Autumn wanted keep it that way.

After a few days away, Aleyah called to check on the girls. Karrie handed the phone to Autumn, "Hey Autumn, how's everything going? Are you and your sister behaving?"

"Yes mom, we're cool. How's your trip?"

"California is amazing, we have to come here for a vacation. I'll be home in a few days. Hold on, Denzel wants to speak with you."

"Mom, no I'd rather not talk…"

Before she could finish her sentence, he was on the phone. "I see that you are still being disobedient. Why don't you do us all a favor and just get out of your mother's life, you're nothing but trouble. Your mother is better off without you, she would be much happier with you gone! You ain't gonna be nothing but a statistic. I know you ain't gonna finish high school because you'll be too busy being pregnant." Autumn didn't respond, she just handed the phone back to Karrie and went into her bedroom, crying and thinking: *'I can't believe that mom lets him treat me that way. How do you watch someone hurt your child? I can't wait to move out. I'll show all of them that I will be successful in everything I do and I definitely won't be having any babies until I get married, fuck Denzel, I hate that bastard!'*

When Aleyah returned home, she came in bearing gifts for everyone except Autumn.

She even had some videos of her and Denzel on all their excursions. While Denzel was giving her a tour of his home he spoke of the people that he missed back in Buffalo and what he missed about them. He associated everyone with characters from the bible, quoting scriptures and what each person represented. At the end of his appreciation speech he looked directly into the camera, *"And then there's the Jezebel, you know who are!"*

Autumn, just shook her head and walked out of the room.

Chapter 20
Summer Breeze

Aleyah heard through the grapevine that Autumn was dating Jorden and the shit hit the fan. She grounded Autumn for a month and forbid her to ever speak to Jorden again. Upon hearing the news, she cried every day and stopped speaking to her mother. To her dismay Aleyah began searching for a new place for her and the girls to move. Despite being locked away in her bedroom for over a week, Autumn came up with a plan to let Jorden know what was going on. She and Brandi's bedroom windows were directly across from each other, so she wrote a letter and had Brandi pass it on to Jorden.

The next afternoon Jorden came knocking at the door and Aleyah answered.

"Hi, I'm Jorden. May I please have a word with you about your daughter?"

"Jorden, I don't see any reason to have this discussion. You are too old to date my daughter."

"I understand why you feel that way, but I am in love with Autumn. I genuinely care for her and I'm not trying to get in her pants, I want her heart."

"No matter what you say Jorden, the fact remains that Autumn is too young for you and she's too young to date. I don't want to see you around my daughter again or I will call the police on you." She slammed the door in his face.

Aleyah was already in a bad mood because she had been trying to contact Denzel for several weeks but could only get his voicemail. After a few months she gave up and then ran into one of his relatives who told her that Denzel was engaged - she was devastated. The news hit her like a ton of bricks. She couldn't believe how Denzel had played her like a fool and broke her heart. She hated men at that point. Like Autumn, trust had now become foreign to her. Men would approach her everywhere she went, but she wouldn't give them the time of day. Aleyah needed some time to heal. Her heart had just been fractured.

Aleyah and the girls were out shopping for their new home when they ran into Blake, a childhood friend of Aleyah's. Blake secretly had a crush on her and felt that seeing her again was the perfect opportunity to ask her out. She accepted his invite to dinner, and to her surprise, Blake blew her mind. He was a true gentleman. After a few dates it was evident that they were in love.

From the start he was a breath of fresh air to Autumn. He was a kind man who was a natural provider and protector to those he loved. Blake knew exactly how to keep Aleyah and her girls happy. Blake had been a friend of the family for years. When he was around they felt safe and Autumn trusted him. That was something that was rare to her. Blake was in the "street pharmaceutical" business, so he had deep pockets and was generous with his fortune. Aleyah loved this.

He kept Aleyah occupied, she seemed to always be at his place and didn't force the girls to come along. Naomi and Autumn would be at home alone all the time, which they loved. New neighbors moved in downstairs, a family of three; two girls and their mother. Their names were Noelle and

Paris. Noelle and Autumn grew close quickly, they were the same age and had a lot in common. Their mom Kelly was easy going with a fun personality. Kelly was also pregnant with twin boys at the time, so she was always in the bed or with the twin's father, at his home. The four girls were free to do whatever they chose with both mothers always away with their men.

The summer after the twins were born was the best. Both Aleyah and Kelly were away the entire summer with their men. Blake made sure that the freezer was full of food and that the girls had money in their pockets. This was perfect because the girls hosted several summer parties where all the kids from the neighborhood would come by and hang out. The older kids would buy liquor and weed and Autumn and Noelle would cook. Being intoxicated and having sexual experienced friends started to peak Autumn's interest. Having both Noelle and Brandi in her ear explaining how good and fun sex was, Autumn was tempted to see for herself. She wanted to lose her virginity to someone who was deserving of her. Jorden came to mind, but after her mother threatened him with the police he never came back around. Autumn learned from Brandi that Jorden had enlisted into the Army and had just completed boot camp. She was sad but was at peace with it. She remembered what Papa-J once said, "if you love something let it go and if it comes back, than it's yours to keep!"

That was the summer when Autumn met Chase. She had seen him around the neighborhood a few times but they never spoke. A mutual friend introduced the two, and once they met there was an instant connection. Chase was an innocent and shy guy, but he was attentive and thoughtful. There was something about Autumn that made him feel comfortable enough to open up and express himself.

He was a breath of fresh air to Autumn. Most guys her age were mannish and had raging hormones. Their way of expressing interest in a girl would be to grab her butt or tell her how fine her body was. Chase was different. He would call Autumn with a song playing in the background and not say a word until the song ended. They would engage in long conversations until the sun came up. He also expressed how he felt by writing Autumn love letters and poems. Another thing that separated him from the rest of the boys was that he didn't mention sex at all. Getting to know Autumn was his true objective, so she gave him her full attention. He made her feel like a princess, always keeping a smile on her face.

By the middle of the new school year Autumn was in love with Chase and she wanted to show him her gratitude. She felt that it was a good time to explore her sexual feelings which had consumed her mind and her body. She grabbed the phone and called Chase, "Can you come over? I need you," said Autumn.

"Is everything okay baby?" he asked.

"Just come over. I need to show you something."

"Okay baby, calm down. I'll be right over," he said.

Autumn hurried into the shower. After she got out she slowly rubbed lotion on her body, then sprayed it down with Aleyah's "Love Spell" by Victoria's Secret. When

Chase knocked on the door she opened it wearing a robe with a pink silk panty and bra set underneath. His jaw fell to the floor as he gazed at her young beautiful body.

"Autumn baby, what's up?"

"Chase, I'm ready to take our relationship to the next level. I want to explore my sexual desires with you."

"Are you sure that you're ready for this? Baby, I'm happy with the way things are. There is no pressure to have sex."

"I want you to be the one to take my virginity, I want to feel you inside of me as we become one."

"If you're sure, then I would be honored."

Autumn led Chase in into the dimly lit apartment, both of their hearts seemed to be beating a little faster. When they got to the sofa Chase sat down as Autumn straddled his lap and began planting soft kisses on his lips, neck and ears. He was aroused immediately. Instead of staying there he picked her up and carried her to the bed. Once they got there he slowly took off her panties and bra while kissing her body. He lay on top of her staring straight into her eyes.

"Are you sure that you want to do this?" he asked.

"Yes, make me a woman baby!"

With the sound of *112's 'Anywhere'* playing in the background Chase took his time penetrating her. He wanted to make her first time as meaningful and painless as possible. With each gentle stroke he stared into her eyes watching her facial expressions. At first she was tense because the first few strokes were piercing, but after a few moments she relaxed and hiked up her legs so he could go deeper. She began feeling warm and tingly all over, the more he stroked, the deeper she was falling for him. All she could think about was how much she loved him and hoped that he'd stay with her forever. The feeling grew mutual between them. He hoped that she was enjoying his loving as he poured it all into her, he wanted her to know that she'd always own his heart. At that heated moment, they both exploded with ecstasy.

After they were finished making love they laid in silence holding each other. Autumn had no idea that her first consensual sexual encounter would unleash something she didn't realize existed in her - a sexual demon.

Chapter 21
Out of the Closet the Skeletons Fell

Chase had gone away to basketball camp for the summer and Autumn missed him terribly. As she sat watching TV there was a knock on her door. Brandi was standing there when she answered. "What's up girl? Come on in."

Brandi quickly walked in with a smile on her face.

"What are you smiling about?" asked Autumn.

"Jorden is back in town!"

"Girl, don't play with me!"

"He gave me his number to pass on to you."

After Brandi left, Autumn sat and stared at the number for twenty minutes before calling him. Her mind kept running back to Chase, but he was away. She thought to herself, *'It won't hurt to just call him.'* That call turned into a three-hour conversation, which turned into a visit that ended with a kiss. All the former feelings had come rushing back and Autumn couldn't resist. It didn't help that she had a new getaway. During the spring Brandi and her mom moved across town so Jorden would visit Autumn over there. Jackie didn't seem to mind so they milked it. Although her mother forbid her to see him, she needed someone to fill Chase's void.

The girls took turns spending the night at each other's house. It was Brandi's turn to stay at Autumn's. She introduced Brandi to her friends from the neighborhood. Tobias who lived a few houses away, had a reputation for being a man whore and it wasn't long after Autumn introduced Brandi and Tobias that they were getting it on.

Their first encounter was on the side of Autumn's house on the door. Later that week Brandi was introduced to Tobias' friend Andre. Brandi also liked Andre and sure enough, she began sleeping with the both of them. When the guys found out they turned their love triangle into a ménage a trios'.

Autumn and Noelle-her neighbor who lived downstairs, were sitting on the porch when Autumn's cousin Larone, who was dating Noelle at the time, came by. He asked if the girls had heard the rumor about Brandi. They both shook their heads no.
"I saw Brandi fucking both Tobias and Andre!" he snickered.
"Where did you see that?" Asked Autumn.
"In Tobias backyard on the picnic table."
Noelle and Autumn were shocked, not so much at her actions, but they wondered why she chose to do in broad daylight. Autumn immediately called Brandi's cell

to warn her that her name had been floating in streets. Brandi panicked as she wondered how to keep Larone from letting more people know about her secret.

Brandi and Autumn began their plot. They had to come up with a plan to bribe Larone so he would keep Brandi's scandalous secret from getting to her parents. Larone was very crafty and tried to make a deal with Brandi. In exchange for his secrecy, she would have to pay him by sucking his dick for a month. Brandi was furious and refused to bow down to him. Larone laughed and told Brandi he would tell his aunt Aleyah if she didn't comply. They hoped that Larone was bluffing but to their horror, he wasn't.

When Aleyah got word about Brandi, she yelled for Autumn to come into the house. "What the hell is going on with Brandi?" She asked.
"Why am I hearing that she's having sex with two guys OUTSIDE?"
Autumn acted as if she knew nothing about the situation, but her mother didn't buy her story. She ended their conversation by telling Autumn that she was going to speak with Brandi's mother, Jackie.

Autumn's first thought was to look for Brandi but of course, she was in the middle of another sexual encounter.

After searching for more than two hours, Autumn found Brandi leaving her latest conquest's house.

"Brandi what are you doing over here? Our mothers are on the phone talking right now, let's go!"

The girls thought of every possible lie they could tell, but it was their word against Larone's.

There were several teenagers hanging out with Autumn on her front porch when Brandi's parents drove up. Jackie jumped out of the car before her dad could put the car into park. "Get your trifling ass over here! You're acting like a little hoe?"

"Can we talk about this at home?" asked Brandi.

"Hell no! Ya trifling ass ain't do it at home!" She slapped Brandi upside the head and her dad yanked her by the shirt and pushed her into the car. Brandi was in tears with both of her parents yelling at the top of their lungs as the car drove off.

Everyone sat there in a state of shock for a while. A minute later they all busted out into laughter. Just when Autumn thought it was safe to laugh, her mother called her in the house. Jackie, felt obligated to let

Aleyah know that Autumn wasn't innocent either.

Jackie had told her mother all about the visits with Jorden. Considering that Jorden and Autumn hadn't been physically intimate at all, besides kissing, it wasn't that bad. However, Aleyah was still disappointed because she had forbid them to see each other. She had been around the block and knew Jorden was after more than just her daughter's conversation. Autumn was not as naïve as Aleyah thought because she never allowed Jorden the chance to sample her goodies. Autumn was grounded for a week.

Her punishment ended when her mother took her to the hair salon. Aleyah was just grateful that her daughter wasn't as loose as Brandi and realized that what she did wasn't so bad after all. A week after her punishment was over, Jorden was due to report back for duty in the Army. They didn't have a chance to say goodbye, but him leaving was perfect timing because Chase would soon be home.

Chapter 22
Her Sweet Scent Blew in the Air

When Chase came back from camp he got word that Autumn and Jorden had been seen hanging out. As soon as he hooked up with Autumn he didn't hesitate to ask if what he had heard was true. Autumn couldn't lie, she told Chase the truth. This crushed him and their relationship. She walked away hurt but, at least she walked away with her dignity.

She decided to take some time off from dating because she needed to clear her mind. Having lost so many loves so early in life, she needed time to breathe.

Beginning with her father, then Jorden and now Chase, she was left wondering why every man she loves leaves her? It was time to make some changes and focus her energy on something different.

Now fifteen, Autumn began looking for a job. She landed a job working in a hair salon as a shampoo girl for one of the ladies at her church, Giselle. It was the change she needed. Giselle paid her fifty dollars a week and Autumn could get her hair done as often as she liked. In addition, Giselle would take her shopping and give her great advice. She was like a big sister to Autumn and they grew very close quickly. Giselle was seven years older than Autumn, but always treated Autumn as if they were the same age. This was exactly the type of guidance she needed. Giselle was someone who could teach her valuable things that she could use in her everyday life.

Autumn was running errands for the salon when she ran into a friend from school who told her that his homeboy Edwin had been asking about her. At that time she wasn't interested in him or anyone else. A few weeks later, out the blue, she received a call from Edwin who lived in Virginia. He wanted to know if they could hang out when he came to visit Buffalo. She said yes, but after they hung up the phone, she forgot about him.

Six months had gone by and Autumn was blossoming by the day. She was now a freshman at a vocational high school where she majored in business. Her mentality was different. She was developing into a young woman who was working and growing both mentally and physically. The fact that she was also very beautiful didn't hurt either. With her beauty, Autumn became very popular with the guys and very unpopular with the girls in school. In short, they hated her guts. Through it all she remained positive because for the first time in her life, she felt that all was well and she was finally in control.

It was the day of the salon's picnic and Autumn had a great time hanging out with the ladies, who were all older than her. They took a special interest in her, schooling her on the ways of men and life's many challenges.

When she got home there was a nice surprise waiting on her porch - Edwin - who stood six feet, Puerto Rican with jet-black hair and a beautiful smile. Autumn was mesmerized, but she played it cool. Thanks to her new friends at the salon, she knew exactly how to make men putty in her hands. Autumn and Edwin sat on the porch and talked all night until the sun came up. Edwin left her with a sweet taste in her mouth; he was charming, intelligent and gorgeous. She wasn't sure where things would go, but she definitely enjoyed his company.

The next day Edwin surprised Autumn at the salon with flowers. "*Awww,*" screamed the women in the salon in unison as Autumn blushed. He continued to impress and after her shift ended, Edwin took Autumn to the park, where he had a blanket set out with rose petals, candles and a basket of food.

Edwin and Autumn hit it off and started dating immediately. They spent every day together and soon became intimate. Edwin truly unleashed the freak in Autumn. He taught her the importance of different positions with an emphasis on her being on top. He also had Autumn performing oral sex like a well-seasoned pro. While she did have a little experience, her appetite for sex had taken a much higher plane. They went at it morning, noon and night, and since her mother was hardly ever home, it was always possible. Autumn and Edwin were like a couple of jackrabbits; they would have sex wherever they could, outside, inside, upstairs, downstairs, on the stairs. Edwin had her addicted to his loving and spontaneity, he lived on the edge and she enjoyed the adventure.

Edwin felt so comfortable being with Autumn that he invited her to join him and his family on a road trip to Toronto for the Caribana. Aleyah was skeptical, so she told Autumn that the only way she could go was if her and Naomi could tag along. Edwin's parents agreed.

Caribana is an event Toronto hosts every year. It's a Caribbean Carnival event that has been billed as North America's largest street festival. People walk from block to block eating, talking and laughing while enjoying all of the festivities of the day. After being there for a few hours, Edwin and Autumn told their parents that they were tired from all of the walking and wanted to head to the car to rest for a while. Truthfully, they wanted to be alone.

As they walked back toward the car, it began to rain. They quickly ran to the doorway of an abandoned building to get out of the rain. As they stood watching the rain fall, chills went through Autumns' body and suddenly the entire scene became sexy. Their eyes locked, then passionate kisses followed. Moments later they were on the side of the building making love. Autumn felt a sense of freedom, spontaneity and love.

These teenagers were head over heels for each other, but it all soon came to a halt when Edwin had to move back to Virginia because he and his father didn't get along. Autumn was devastated. Before they parted ways, he explained that he was in love with her and wanted to marry her when he came back to Buffalo. She was excited, but didn't realize they were too young for marriage.

Once they arrived at the Airport it became real that he was leaving. The one person she felt comforted by and the one person who helped free her spirit was flying back to Virginia. Once again, Autumn was overwhelmed with loneliness.

Chapter 23
Creating Her Identity

After Edwin left Autumn needed to get her mind off of him. Attention was coming her way, which meant lots of drama as well. She remained driven and couldn't allow the drama nor the loneliness to consume her. She was determined to make something of her life. The hateful words Denzel spoke still rang loudly in her ears and she was determined to beat the statistics. Autumn had heard about the 70% of high school dropouts and the unsolicited teenage pregnancies. She wanted to be different and understood that she had to surround herself by people who dreamed of success.

Every Friday there would be a Pep Rally, it was one of the biggest events at the local High school. The Drill Team and Cheerleading Team would perform while the basketball and football teams were recognized. Autumn was intrigued, she had always wanted to be a part of a team and she believed joining an extra-curricular activity would be a good move for her. After the drill team performed she knew that was where she belonged. They rocked the stage with their racy routine and the crowd went wild.

The next week, try-outs were held and Autumn was there, excited and eager to learn. She did exceptionally well, surprising herself as well as her peers by how quickly she learned the routines. Autumn moved so gracefully, like it was natural to her. Impressed with Autumns talent, the captains eagerly welcomed her to the team.

Autumn was so proud that she was now a part of a drill team who had placed 1st in the state competitions for 3 years in a row. Making the team helped create her reputation at school. She now had teammates in every grade, paving her way to popularity. The girls in her grade became instant haters, but the boys adored her. Everyone wanted a piece of her, but she wasn't interested in anyone at the school. She was getting it on with an older guy from her church, which she kept confidential.

By the end of the school year Autumn was on the drill team, cheerleading team and dance team, all while holding down her job at the salon. Her popularity landed her invites to attend one prom in her freshman year and two proms her sophomore year. Again, the freshman girls did not appreciate that at all. She was getting way too much attention for their taste. Autumn shook it off and continued to do her thing.

Autumn needed to blow off a little steam so she called up her new "piece" Josh to get her brains fucked out. She had met Josh at church, he was twenty five and fine as hell. She'd always had her eye on him, but never thought he'd give her the time of day. That is until one day he slipped her a note with his number. Josh made Autumn promise not to tell anyone about the affair. He made up an excuse about everyone being jealous and creating trouble for them. The truth is he knew charges could be brought against him for having sex with a Sixteen year old. Autumn fell for it and soon Josh was knocking that young pussy out the box. He was a stone cold freak. He loved eating Autumn's pussy, something that was new to her, but she enjoyed it. Josh also liked his nipples rubbed while she rode his face, which Autumn thought was weird, but she went with it.

As much as she resented her mother for hopping from man to man, she didn't realize that she was following in her mother's footsteps. The difference between the two was that sex was now Autumns' drug, she had to have it, it was her therapy.

As the end of her sophomore year approached, Autumn was shining like the northern star. She was a straight-A student and had been nominated as captain for the drill team as well as the dance team. With her accomplishments came the envy. Girls who pretended to be her friends began plotting to jump her and slice her face with a razor on the last day of school. When she heard the news she immediately went into crazy mode. Soon after she was hit with the harsh reality that it was time to switch classes, two of the three girls, Kristina and Bianca, who plotted to attack her, were in the next class.

Autumn stormed into the room breathing fire as she thought to herself, *'how dare these jealous bitches pretend to be my friend for the entire year, then plan to jump me?'* She was beyond angry, she was pissed. Bianca was the first one to come in. She was unattractive with short unmanageable hair. She didn't dress very well and had a terrible attitude. As she walked to her desk, Autumn walked right up to her, "So, I hear that you jealous bitches are planning to jump me and cut my face up! Why couldn't you be bold enough to fight me yourself? I guess that I'm so intimidating that it takes three of you to beat me down, huh?"

Bianca was completely caught off guard denying everything. "You know that you're my girl, I'm not the one that has a problem with you, it's Kristina," Bianca said. Kristina was a pretty girl, with long hair, but no personality. She had a nice shape but a tomboyish style and didn't put much effort into her appearance. As soon as Bianca mentioned her, Kristina walked into the classroom. When Autumn saw her she walked up to Kristina, "There's the hating bitch I was waiting for! So, you're going to cut my face up, huh? Clean yourself up and embrace the fact that you're a girl! That'll help get you some action! Aww, are you mad because you are a tomboy?" Autumn busted out in laughter which everyone else in the class followed. Embarrassed Kristina wasn't going to stay quiet, "Yea I'm going slice yo ass up bitch! You think that you are all of that!" Autumn giggled, "That's what you came up with sweetie? Obviously, you must think that I am the shit, because you put so much energy into trying to cut me up. I'm just curious as to why I am such a threat to you? Why does it matter that I'm confident in myself? Maybe it's because you're lacking that confidence? That makes sense!"

The teacher walked into a classroom that was filled with chaos. They were so loud that people from other classes were peeking into the room to see what was going on. Another teacher nearby called the principal and security. Both Kristina and Autumn were escorted to the principal's office.
Once they arrived in Principal Daniel's office, they both had a chance to tell their side of the story. Autumn knew she would be all right, she had never been in the Principal's office for any trouble, plus she

was the Drill Team captain. They had just won 1st place in the statewide Drill"O"Rama competition and a trophy.

Kristina on the other hand had been in trouble all year and this incident would probably be the last straw for her. Autumn was given first opportunity to tell her side of the story. She winked at Kristina and then began explaining how Kristina planned to attack her with a razor. Principal Daniels immediately grew outraged, she didn't even allow Kristina to tell her side of the story. Principal Daniels gave Kristina a few choice words and then expelled her for the remainder of the school year. Kristina was baffled and broke down in tears. Autumn sat across the room staring at her with victory in her eyes and a smirk on her face. Principal Daniels then dismissed Autumn, allowing her to go back to class. As she walked back she thought to herself *two down, one to go*. Jessica was next, she was the 3rd plotter in the scheme.

When Autumn went back to class, her peers were buzzing about the argument between her and Kristina. Everyone was surprised that she had an aggressive side, her demeanor was usually sweet and humble and she got along with mostly everybody. Once her other side was revealed, her popularity shot through the roof. She didn't allow it to go to her head though.

Autumn didn't want to make another scene, and being that she got off easy with the principal, she decided to take a different approach with Jessica. She had heard about Autumn confronting the other girls, and was quiet the entire class. This was unusual for a motor mouth like Jessica. Autumn was nonchalant as Jessica tried to apologize. "Save your bullshit, the truth of the matter is that you're fake and I'm not going to waste my energy on you! Get out of my face!" Jessica was speechless and embarrassed.

The last day of class was crazy, again, Autumn heard a rumor that a cousin of one of her Drill Team members was outside waiting to fight her. The girl didn't even attend her school. This stemmed from the girl's boyfriend liking Autumn, but the story had been twisted. Her boyfriend was dating Paris, her downstairs neighbor. The girl and her crew planned to surprise Autumn with a beat down, luckily, she had a heads up. Instead of getting the few friends she had in school to help, she called her mother.

Autumn was no punk but she needed backup. Aleyah arrived with her sister Nina and a few of their cousins waiting in the car. When they walked outside the school she saw Kristina and Jessica waiting. When she looked across the street, she saw five other girls. All seven girls wanted to bust her ass. Aleyah called her cousins out the car. They all stood in the middle of the street facing Autumn's foes. "Anyone who has a problem with my daughter step up! Don't let her pretty face fool you she ain't no punk! I hear ya'll want to fight, so line up. She'll take each one of you straight up! There ain't gonna be none of the jumping bullshit!" shouted Aleyah.

Autumn stood there ready for war while they all stood perplexed - nobody said anything. "Everyone had a problem with me earlier," said Autumn. "And now nobody has anything to say, huh? You girls are some real corny bitches! Get some business about yourselves, because I don't have time for this petty nonsense! I have a future ahead me, while you bitches stay chasing these silly niggas!"

Autumn and her family drove off laughing.

Chapter 24
Life Changing Decisions

Aleyah decided that her family had been through enough, it was time to relocate to a different state. There was a lot going on in the small town of Buffalo; 80% of high school girls were pregnant, or on their 2nd child. 90% of the guys were high school dropouts, drug dealers, and baby daddies. She refused to allow her girls to end up amongst the statistics that continued to plague their town. There weren't enough opportunities for growth.

Autumn was too young to understand that her mother wanted to raise them in a better environment. She couldn't fathom living in a new place where she didn't know anyone. Aleyah had been talking to everyone she knew about moving away. One of her girlfriends had introduced her to an older guy by the name of Dwight. Dwight was visiting from Atlanta and somehow convinced Aleyah that relocating to Atlanta would be a great opportunity for her and the girls. After doing some research of her own she liked what she was hearing about Atlanta. She began planning to move before the beginning of the new school year. She was done with Buffalo and wanted to leave all the bad memories behind.

By September they were ready to go. Aleyah packed their clothes and anything that could fit in their Honda Accord and they drove to Atlanta. The car was so packed that there wasn't even enough room for the girl's feet to touch the floor. Autumn and Naomi cried the entire 13 hour ride. It seemed like torture.

When they finally reached the "Dirty South" the streets seemed oddly familiar; there were drug addicts roaming the streets in search of their next hit, dope boys loitering at the corner stores and prostitutes turning tricks on Candler Rd. Autumn was definitely unimpressed. She was thinking, *'We left home to come to the same shit that we're trying to escape? This is some straight bullshit! Where are all the beautiful lights and buildings everyone talks about?'*

Until they could find a place of their own, they lived with Dwight and his son Niles in Decatur, GA. There were only two bedrooms, so Autumn, Aleyah, and Naomi shared a room. This made things weird and uncomfortable because it was Autumn and Naomi's first time meeting either of these guys.

Dwight was a short, unpleasant man, who was always rude when approaching people. Autumn immediately felt a bad vibe from

Dwight. She knew to keep her distance and protect her sister, because she knew that her mother would not do so. She watched as Dwight treated Niles like a slave. He was always giving orders and yelling at him, he would even make fun of Niles in front of others. This behavior disturbed Autumn.

Niles was twenty one years old. He was very quiet and shy and didn't socialize or have conversations with anyone. It was obvious that his father had destroyed his confidence.

Dwight made it seem as if Niles was mentally challenged, but Autumn wanted to form her own opinion. She decided to build a friendship with Niles, creating a comfort zone for him to be himself. She began making small talk by asking him his interests, hobbies and so forth. It took a little time for him to warm up, but eventually he started to open up. In that time Autumn learned that Niles was a quiet storm, he was searching for the cloud's ending and the sun's beginning.

Niles longed for happiness, something that he hadn't felt in a long time. His dad had been absent from his life up until a year before Aleyah and the girls had arrived. His mother put him out on the streets at sixteen, where he remained for several months before joining the Army, where he served four years. Niles thought he'd finally found happiness; he had a great career, had fallen in love and he was engaged to be married. Unfortunately, things took a turn for the worse when he witnessed his fiancée killed while on the battlefield. This left him devastated. Since then, he had been in a trance. He immediately and indefinitely shut down. Niles allowed others to take advantage of him in order to keep peace. He was in deep need of love from family, friends and the love of a significant other. He wanted desperately to be a part of something so bad that he was willing to sacrifice his own integrity to belong to something. He didn't realize that self-love was most important and without that, there was no way anyone else could love or respect him.

Niles and Autumn grew close over the course of the few months that they lived together. They would hang out while Dwight and Aleyah were working because Niles felt more comfortable that way. After getting him to open up, Autumn grew curious about Niles' love life, she wondered if he had one. She began to inquire about the kind of women he was interested in. At first, he wasn't sure of his type, but eventually he did explain that it had been years since he had been physical with a woman. His fiancée was the last woman he had touched.

"Don't you get horny?" asked Autumn. "I know that men are naturally horny creatures, how do you suppress those feelings?"

"Yeah, I get very horny, but I usually just jack off. I haven't been comfortable enough with a woman to have sex since she died."

Autumn felt bad for him. He was a grown man who hadn't had sex with a woman in years. She decided to take on the role of helping him gain his confidence back. She started by teaching him how to initiate a conversation, discussing how to relax when speaking to people and the importance of eye contact. They practiced that for a few weeks until he was confident in his conversation.

Next on her agenda was teaching Niles about how to approach women. At first he was timid, but eventually he began to get into it and even started asking questions. "Women like a confident man, who's also a gentleman. Look into her eyes, introduce yourself and give her a compliment" she suggested. "Ok, practice on me."

"Hi, I'm Niles and I think that you're beautiful."
"That was great! You were confident and smooth."

They both burst into laughter. "You've been all up in my business, so I have a question for you," said Niles.

"Ok, ask away."

"You've been here for a while, why aren't you seeing anybody?" He questioned.

"I'm not really into these country guys. They're just not my flavor." said Autumn.

"So, you're not horny?"

"Hell yeah, but I'll just have to deal with it until I find someone I like" said Autumn.

"That's understandable. Well, now that you have me curious to learn, can I ask you how to please a woman? I want to know how to make a woman scream." said Niles.

"Wow, I wasn't expecting that. Ok, what exactly do you want to know? Give me details." She said.

"I've always wanted to learn how to eat pussy really well."

Autumn burst into laughter, completely caught off guard. "I apologize for laughing, again I wasn't expecting that. Give me your arm."

Autumn took his arm and demonstrated how to lick a kitty. "First you want to examine it for bumps and check the scent. You don't want to be eating a spoiled pussy."

They both laughed.

"Then gently taste it to make sure it's sweet. Start at the clit, that's where most of the stimulation comes from."

She began licking on his arm to demonstrate how gentle his lick should be. "That feels good," he said. "I can imagine what that feels like down on the kitty"

Autumn extended her arm so that he could practice on her. He did it perfectly.

"Now, lick it in the shape of a figure eight."

Again, he did it perfectly and this time Autumn's pussy began to tingle, so she ended their session for the night.

She went to bed with her body steaming, she hadn't had sex in a couple of months and her hormones were raging. She had been fantasizing about getting fucked since she'd been in Atlanta, but hadn't met anyone that she was sexually attracted to as of yet. She went to sleep frustrated.

After a few days she gave Niles another lesson. She needed her hormones to cool down a bit. Once they talked again he was eager to learn more, he even prepared questions. Autumn was thoroughly impressed by his progress. She could see the confidence in him and this made her proud.

After their conversation that night Autumn felt herself, yet again, getting hot and bothered, so she decided to get in the shower to take off some of the edge. As she washed her body, her pussy pulsated and her mind began to wander. *'If I could just get someone to eat my pussy with no strings attached that would be great! I just need to cum without having to give anything in return. Damn, but what dude would go for that?'*

She got out the shower and went to put on a T-shirt and shorts with no panties. She then sashayed out into the living room where Niles was playing video games. She fought with her devious thoughts and at that moment she realized that she was addicted to sex. She had to have it or her body would explode.

Because she was raised by parents who were both manipulative, Autumn knew exactly how to get what she wanted without actually asking for it. "What's this you're playing?" She asked Niles.

"Mortal Kombat, would you like to play?" He asked.

"I've never played this before. Can you teach me the game?"

Niles happily showed her how to play the game. He was excited that someone else wanted to play with him. During the game she slightly opened her legs, she knew that her scent would travel directly to his nose.

"Can I ask you for a favor?" asked Niles.

"Sure, what's up?"

"Can I eat your pussy? I've been dreaming about it since we talked about it the other night. I want to taste the real thing."

Autumn's pussy almost jumped out of her shorts! "I don't know if that's such a good idea, it will change everything. Plus, our parents are in the next room." She said.
"I just want to taste it, you don't have to do anything to me and I promise things won't change."

Niles leaned forward and Autumn scooted up to his face. He pulled her shorts to the side and began kissing her pussy gently. He took in a deep breath, smelling her scent. "Mmm, it smells so good and taste so sweet." He said as he dove into her sweet pussy, devouring it.

Autumn coached him every step of the way until she exploded in his mouth. Niles loved every moment, sucking her cum up like it was the last drop of water on earth. After she came, she jumped up and ran into the bathroom to wash up. *'I can't believe I just seduced this poor dude for my selfish gain.'* She thought.

Chapter 25
Silence Can Be So Loud!

By November Aleyah found a townhouse for her family to move in to. Autumn was excited to move away from Dwight, he was such a scrooge. Having their own space was a breath of fresh air for all of them. It gave them a chance to really settle into Atlanta and see what it had to offer.

Autumn was trying to adjust to a new school in her junior year. She didn't make many girlfriends because her presence made a statement that girls disliked. By this time she had come to terms with woman hating her, it became motivational. The boys, on the other hand, loved her. This was not a surprise, she was a fresh, pretty face with a captivating personality. The boys couldn't resist and she didn't repel the attention. Real New Yorkers just played the hand they're dealt. All they received from her was conversation and a smile. Another challenge for her was learning the Dirty South slang. Everyone spoke with deep country accents and called each other "shawty".

Niles started coming by the new house to visit Aleyah and the girls, he had gotten used to having them around, especially since he lived with the scrooge. He mentioned that Dwight was bad mouthing Aleyah and the girls, particularly Autumn. Dwight made a remark in regards to Autumn suggesting that she had been pregnant before because young girls her age don't have huge breast like that. This offended Niles because he had developed feelings for her. He, however, didn't share these feelings with anyone.

Grateful for his loyalty, Aleyah offered Niles an open invitation to come over whenever he needed a break from Dwight. This included overnight visits. That was music to Autumn's ears as her pussy tingled. It had been months since Niles had the luxury of tasting her. She fought with herself about getting involved with Niles because she was still learning the power of her pussy and she didn't want poor Niles falling in love with her. He was not her type, plus she was sure that her mother wouldn't approve.

...

Being in a new state began to take its toll. Naomi and Autumn rarely attended school and when Aleyah noticed the change in their moods she didn't pressure them to go. They would spend their days in the house watching T.V and eating. Eventually, Autumn grew tired of being nonproductive, so she decided to go back to school. It took a lot out of her to adjust to all the changes. She became depressed having too much free time and her mind often wandered.

When she was in Buffalo she always had things to do and friends to hang out with. By staying busy she didn't have to deal with her pain. Now her past was catching up with her. She was faced with the mirror image of the young girl who had become a sex object. She had buried this part of her life, but it was starting to resurface, like a dead man floating in the sea.

One morning Autumn was waiting for the school bus to arrive. As she stood there she started hearing voices in her head. *'Jump out in the middle of the road. You don't deserve to live. You are a filthy and disgusting whore. You aren't worthy of love. There is no reason for you to live.'*

The voices began invading her thoughts daily. She spent many sleepless nights having nightmares about being raped and waking up in cold sweats. Autumns' emotions were all over the place. She felt as if she had nothing to offer, other than sex. What she didn't realize, is that she had been brainwashed to think that way. She was so mentally unstable that her life had become a blur. She felt empty and unworthy as the voices in her head haunted her. Again, she shared her thoughts with no one. She wanted to deal with this alone, out of fear that nobody would understand. Her family would surely think she was crazy. Autumn even contemplated suicide in order to shut off the voices in her mind and the shame she felt. Aleyah saw the depression in her daughter, but ignored it, assuming that it would go away. One day she came home early from school, and wrote a suicide note for her mother.

Dear Mom,

I hate who I've become. My very being is a disgrace. I live with emptiness, a void that can't be filled and I'm tired of being in this place. Not even my own mother will help me shed the demons that haunt me every day. I can no longer live with this pain. It is my time to pass away. I want out of this life, which has caused me nothing but misery. I am continuously asking if anybody in this world loves me. I will make it easier on everybody by taking my life, that way you all never have to deal with me for the rest of your lives.

Love,
Autumn

Autumn, tied a rope around her neck and stood on a chair, trying to choke herself to death. She lost oxygen quickly to her brain, but she couldn't go through with it because she knew this was completely insane.

Naomi came to mind and it made her cry, so she untied her neck, fell to the floor and began crying even more. "What the fuck am I doing? What if my baby sister finds me? I can't have this on my conscience forever haunting me."

She dropped to her knees and began to pray, asking God to take her ill thoughts away. She made it through that day, but those demons were not done playing with her head.

A few days later as Autumn waited for the school bus, the demons came back with a vengeance, telling her to jump out in front of the moving cars *'Now is a good time to end it all, it'll look like an accident.'* She closed her eyes and stuck one foot off the curb into oncoming traffic and inches away from ending her life. Suddenly the wind knocked her backwards, away from the curb. It was in that moment that she heard God's voice louder than ever before. He told her that it was time to confront her fears before they defeated her and that he would hold her hand through it all.

Chapter 26
Chasing Waterfalls

It was Valentine's Day, the season for love all over the world and Autumn was a little sad because she didn't have anyone special to share it with. To her surprise, when she reached her locker, there was a rose attached to a card - she had a secret admirer. She had no clue that someone had a crush on her.

Autumn went to her first period class and took her seat. Jerome, a boy in her class came in with a huge bear, a card and some candy, and then placed it on her desk. She was flattered again, having no idea that

Jerome thought of her enough to buy a Valentine's Day gift. The day just kept getting better and better, and by the end of the school day, she had received gifts from guys in each of her classes! She had so many gifts that she couldn't carry her books! To no surprise, envy came from all the girls and she loved every second of it - the jealousy from them flattered her as well.

Jerome asked Autumn out that evening. She thought he was a nice guy, attractive with a great body, but there were some things that concerned Autumn about him. He had a few feminine tendencies that she noticed a while back. Nonetheless, she took him up on his offer and figured that at the least, they could be good friends.

Autumn began hanging out with Jerome frequently, he was the first guy that had her interest in the "dirty south". He was cool and fun to go dancing with, he was a great dancer, something she was great at as well. After being friends for several months he expressed his feelings for her and they began dating. Autumn was ecstatic that her mother approved of him.

One day they were hanging out at Jerome's watching a movie when he leaned in for a kiss. Passionately, he grabbed the back of Autumn's head and slowly stuck his tongue in her mouth. As their tongues danced, so did Autumn's pussy. The chemistry was on point and the moment was right. He turned on 'Freak Me' by Silk and laid her down on his bed, still kissing her and not missing a beat. He undressed her and began to kiss every inch of her body, working his way down to her 'love below' Jerome kissed her pussy lips and then gently slid his tongue down her lips to open her up. Autumn was impressed with his skills. He licked her kitty like a lollipop and she was dripping wet. Then he undressed, revealing his incredible body, with six-pack abs and a tight chest. Autumn couldn't resist kissing his body, it was just too beautiful. When he took off his underwear unleashing his huge dick, Autumn's eyes opened wide. *'Damn, it's been 8 months since these walls had any penetration'* she thought. *'A sexy body and a big dick - it's on!'* she thought.

Autumn asked him for a condom, she was horny as hell, but no fool. She watched him slide it on his dick and then she mounted him. She rode his dick into ecstasy, watching his eyes roll to the back of his head as he moaned her name. She enjoyed watching him go crazy. She thought to herself, *'I'm a bad bitch, I wonder if he can handle this pussy.'* As soon as she thought that, he flipped her over onto her back and began stroking her pussy at a nice steady rhythm. Jerome had technique; he was switching up the positions with smooth moves and not missing a beat. Then, he put Autumn on all fours, hitting it doggy-style, deep stroking and long stroking so gently. Her body began shaking uncontrollably which ended in a puddle on Jerome's bed. She was so embarrassed because she had made such a mess, this had never happened before. As she apologized Jerome explained to her that she had her first orgasm. *'Damn, I came? After all the sexing I've done? He's the first one to make me cum?'* she thought. Yes, she'd experienced small orgasms while receiving oral sex, but not resulting in puddles of her wetness like this!

That was the first of many orgasms Jerome gave Autumn. Every chance they had, they would fuck. He was in so deep, that he couldn't take it. His feelings for her began to take a toll on him as he would think about her all day, then dream about her at night. He was losing control, something that he never felt before. Even his mother noticed the change in him and advised him to see other girls because she knew that Autumn was too much for her son. Autumn was built like a woman, with curves and a beautiful face and his mother despised her very presence. Although Jerome was feeling overwhelmed, he just couldn't let go, She had a hold on him.

It wasn't until the day of their junior prom that the universe drove a wedge between them. Autumn had an early appointment to get her hair done, and after the appointment, she, Aleyah, and Jerome headed downtown to underground Atlanta to do some last minute shopping. Autumn was famished from running errands all day, so she and Jerome stopped at the KFC on the corner of Capital Avenue while her mother went across the street to shop for Autumn's accessories.

They had been shopping for over 3 hours and Autumn grew exhausted, not to mention she was anxiously anticipating the night. They ordered their food and sat down to eat. A junkie walked over to ask if they were interested in watching a card trick. She rejected, but the junkie was really persistent. As the he proceeded with his tricks, Autumn and Jerome ate their food. She didn't realize that she had placed her change and receipt from the food on the table alongside her bags. As she looked down to grab her chicken the junkie snatched her money and took off running. Autumn looked over at Jerome in disbelief, also to see what he was going to do about it. He looked just as surprised as her, but then looked away in shame.

She immediately jumped up from the table and chased the junkie around the corner. She and the junkie ended up in an alley arguing. "Give me back my damn money!" yelled Autumn.

"Bitch, I'm not giving you shit! I won this money!"

"I was not playing the game with you. Give me back my money right now!" she demanded.

As she checked the scenery to see if there was anyone around that could help, reality had set in. She was arguing with a man who was clearly on drugs, in the middle of an alley. There was no one in sight, not even her supposed-to-be "boyfriend"

Jerome. The junkie started jumping at Autumn, as if he was going to hit her. "Bitch, I'll kick your teeth out your mouth, if you don't get the fuck out of my face!" threatened the junkie.

"I'm not going anywhere until you give me my damn money. Try me if you like, I'll kick your crack head ass!" She shouted back.

The junkie stared at Autumn with a stunned look on his face, then he took the money out of his pockets, ripped one of her twenty dollar bills, and then threw the money to the ground. She was afraid to bend down to pick it up, in fear that he would actually kick her in the face. She prayed and moved quickly, grabbing the money off the ground, as he took off running.

After the junkie was out of sight Autumn removed the mask of strength and fearlessness, revealing her true feelings of terror and loneliness. Tears began to run down her face and all she could think of was, *'I can't believe that Jerome did not have my back, where the fuck was he? He wasn't man enough to stand up for his girl? Oh No! I don't deal with punk ass niggas!'*

As she headed back toward KFC crying hysterically, Jerome came around the corner.

"What happened?" He asked.

"Get the hell out of my face, you punk ass nigga! Where the fuck were you? I'm out here arguing with a crack head and you're inside KFC eating? What kind of shit is that? What type of guy would let his lady go out there by herself!"

He stood silently, looking ashamed.
"Yeah, I thought so! Not a man at all! She snapped. "You are a punk and I don't deal with coward ass men! How is it that I have more heart than you? The least that you could have done was stand by my side, just in case he jumped on me. Truth be told you should have been the one out here getting my money back. I should have been the

one standing at YOUR side. That's a damn shame! What a man!" yelled Autumn.

As they reached the corner, Aleyah was crossing the street, walking toward them.

"What's wrong?" She asked.

"A crack head stole my money! I had to go get it back from him myself, because this punk ass nigga was afraid! He didn't even come outside with me while I was out here arguing with the crack head to get it back! I'll say it again, I can't stand a man who's a punk!"

Aleyah looked at Jerome in disbelief as she tried to calm her daughter down.

"I didn't want to leave all of our stuff in KFC." He said.

"Is that the best that you could come up with? Screamed Autumn. "You are so pitiful! You make me sick!"

Autumn was pissed and there were no words to describe how she felt at the time. All she knew was that she no longer wanted to be in his presence and she definitely didn't want to go to the prom with him. Prom night was supposed to be exciting, not dramatic. Besides, who wants to be seen at the prom with a guy who was a bitch?

Aleyah insisted that she quiet down and rethink her decision about not going to the prom with Jerome. It was the one day Autumn had put a lot into and she did not want all the hard work to be in vain, so she just bit the bullet and went anyway.

Autumn wore a beautiful royal blue and white gown made with valor material. She had an up-do that was exquisite and French manicured nails. Plus, there was a stretch limo waiting to take them to prom. After a few hours, she calmed down and said to herself, *'Have a good time tonight, but after the prom, I'm done.'*

This was the third prom Autumn had attended, so she wasn't impressed this time around. The night was decent, but she didn't enjoy the festivities of the evening. Once it was over, the teenagers who rode in the stretch limo wanted to hang out, but

Autumn went home. She didn't want to be bothered with anyone.

As Jerome walked Autumn to the door she turned to him and said "My perception of you has changed Jerome. This just isn't going to work. We've had some fun, but I believe that our time is up."

His face hit the ground and his heart followed. Before he could respond, Autumn walked inside the house and closed the door. To her surprise Niles was sitting in the living room watching a movie. His eyes nearly popped out of his head when he saw how beautiful she looked, all dressed up in her gown. "Oh hey Niles, you scared me." She said. He was speechless.

Autumn waved her hand in the air, across his eyes for him to snap out of his trance. "I-I'm sorry" he stuttered. "It's just that you look amazing. I was caught off guard."
"Thank you, I just came back from prom." She said.
"How was it? I've never been to one before."
"It was ok, nothing fancy. Maybe it's because this is my third prom."
"Wow, you must be really popular. Give me all the details, please." He begged.
"Let me get out of this dress and I'll be right back to tell you about it."

"Alright, I'll be waiting."

As Autumn changed her clothes her pussy began to tingle with sensation. The thought of Niles sliding his tongue in and out of her wetness felt naughty, but nice. Her mind began racing, *'Damn, I'm horny and mom isn't home… No, this is wrong, I'm just going to chill and talk.'*

As she painted him a picture of what prom is like, her mind just wouldn't back down and her pussy pulsated at a rapid pace while her juices began to flow. Her sweet scent traveled directly into Niles's nostrils. He too was fantasizing about having Autumns' sweetness on his lips. It had been a while since their last encounter when Autumn freaked out on him, so he was afraid to make a move.

Autumn couldn't calm her crazy kitten so she went into the kitchen to make a snack. As she made her sandwich, Niles quietly walked up behind her, got on his knees and slowly slid her shorts off, then licked her pussy from the back. Autumn was in shock by his bold move, but she was incredibly turned on. This was her first time getting eaten from the back, naughty thoughts flew through her mind so she ran with it. "Mmmm, I like that, you're doing it so good baby." She purred.

"You taste so sweet - I've been going through withdrawals without you." Said Niles.

"Oh yeah? How bad do you want this pussy?" She questioned as she pulled her pussy off his lips, teasing, rubbing her ass and kitty across his face. Niles melted at the sound of her voice, she had a spell on him so deep it was evident that he wanted to be her sex slave. "I want it so bad," he said. "It's like my drug, I can't function without it. Give it to me, let me taste it."

Autumn bent over and touched her toes. "Eat my pussy." She demanded as she spread her kitty lips wide open. "Stick your tongue in the hole. Yes, just like that. Now lick my ass. Oh yeah, that's good!" She had become a qualified seductress in that moment and there was no turning back. She enjoyed having the power of turning a man into putty.

As she climaxed on his face she thought '*I have to add ass licking to my sexual menu*'. Niles didn't even realize what he had just started and since she was now single, she needed someone to fulfill her sexual appetite. He could fill the void until she found someone new.

Chapter 27
Getting Dirty In the "Dirty Dirty"

Autumn received a letter in the mail stating that some of her high school credits didn't transfer from New York State because Georgia's school systems were different. She had two options, either repeat her junior year or attend a Credit Restoration school called Open Campus. If she attended Open Campus, she would have a chance to make up her credits and graduate on time. So naturally Autumn decided to attend Open Campus, she had worked too hard to keep a 4.0 average to be held back a year. Walking across that stage dressed in a cap and gown was something that she looked forward to, and nothing was going to stand in her way.

Senior year began and the pressure was on. Autumn adjusted to her new schedule right away, it was perfect for her. Classes were in six week increments and the protocol stressed that students weren't allowed to miss more than five classes per quarter and students could come and go as they pleased, as long as their class work was completed. This worked well because she was a fast learner.

Autumn met a lot of interesting people there, some of who showed her how to have some real fun in the "dirty south".

Autumns' new friends turned her onto smoking weed, which the country boys called "trees". She loved the way weed made her forget about all the bullshit in her life. It kept her mind at ease. She figured, as long as getting high didn't affect her 4.0 average, she was free to do as she pleased.

Autumn's entire perception began to change when she saw what Atlanta had to offer. As she took a look around the city she renamed "The Black Come Up". It became clear to her that people of color could be successful too. Blacks in the south were doing their thing, they owned nice homes and drove nice cars and having great credit was something that was rare where Autumn came from. An amazing feeling came over her. As she began envisioning her own dreams, she realized that she too could be successful. Autumn pictured herself in sexy business suits working for prestigious companies that offered benefit packages. Only seventeen at the time, she hit the pavement in search for a job. She figured, *'What the hell, I have to start somewhere.'*

Autumn landed a job working for "Rainbow" a women's clothing store in Avondale Mall. It wasn't the office over the city, but she was doing something she enjoyed, which was shop while she worked. The holiday season had rolled around and the store was very busy, everyone was out shopping for their loved ones.

This particular evening, Autumn was working the cash register when she had an older gentlemen customer. It was very odd to see a man of his age and style shopping in a woman's clothing store like Rainbow. When he reached the register she was pleasant, giving him good customer service with her signature smile. He gave her a look as if he had just seen an angel. She smiled and continued to ring up his merchandise. He began showering her with compliments until she turned red. Once his purchase was complete, she said, "Thank you and Happy Holidays."

The older gentlemen introduced himself as William Blue and slid Autumn a business card, along with a twenty dollar bill. She immediately explained to him that it was against company policy to accept tips. He cut her off as he placed his hand atop of hers saying that it was not a tip, but a small percentage of what she could have if she were to become his Sugar baby. Autumn's eyes nearly popped out of her head. William Blue could read her expression, so he then told her to consider his offer and to give him a call once she made a decision.

Again, she just smiled at him, totally speechless. It wasn't because he gave her money, but his proposition. Autumn had always heard of Sugar Daddies, but never had the opportunity to have one. Thoughts of shopping sprees, jewelry and cars floated through her mind. She was no fool though, she knew that in life you never get something for nothing, so she was curious to find out what that something was.

A few days later, Autumn arrived a little early to work to get ready for her shift. As she walked into the mall, William greeted her with a thousand dollars cash in his hands. "Call into work and spend the day with me. I'll compensate you for your time missed. All this could be yours if you just walk out of the door with me" said William Blue.

Autumn immediately became conscience of how crazy this man was. Thoughts of being kidnapped, chopped into pieces and her body disposed of in the woods ran through her brain. She declined his offer. She simply explained that there would be no one to cover her shift. William was extremely frustrated as he threw his wealth in her face, "I could take care of you, if you let me, you don't need this bullshit job. You're too good to work here, so why don't you quit and let me handle everything you need?"

William was more than Autumn could handle and he became aggressive when she wasn't receptive to his offer as he planned. Autumn politely declined once again. William was fed up by that point and stormed off as he yelled, "It's your loss not mine!"

'Bullshit! She thought to herself. *'Baby I'm a winner, that's why you're mad.'*
William would occasionally shop in the mall, stalking Autumn on the low, but she kept her distance and her eyes open. Finally he got the picture and she never saw him again.

When inventory came back with bad numbers, Corporate cleaned the store out. The store would soon be getting a brand new staff and everyone was fired except for Autumn. She praised GOD. The new manager hired an entire new staff, including two storage room employees who were in charge of putting out all new merchandise. One of the guys was named Taylor. He was tall and goofy, but he was nice. Taylor immediately took an interest in Autumn. He would ask her out every time they saw each other, but Taylor had corny pickup lines and jokes, so she would gently turn him down every time.

Never one to give up, Taylor began writing Autumn notes quoting Shakespeare and after countless attempts, Autumn finally agreed to have lunch with him. Although he wasn't her type of guy, she gave him a chance. He impressed her with his mannerisms and generosity and after hanging out a few times, he began to grow on her.

Taylor was the epitome of a southern gentleman; he treated Autumn with respect, he would open doors and pull out chairs for her - making her feel like a queen. She had never experienced this type of treatment with any of her past boyfriends and she soon fell for the tall, goofy guy who she would have never taken a second look at.

Both teenagers were approaching the end of their senior year of high school. Although Autumn struggled with her math class, she was doing exceptionally well in rest of her classes. That one class had her in danger of not graduating on time. She panicked about being left behind, that was something she had been dealing with her entire life and she was not about to be the one responsible for failing. She had just applied to Georgia State and planned on majoring in psychology. She was determined to be successful. Proving Denzel wrong had become an obsession.

Chapter 28
Changing lanes

The store manager at Rainbow began cutting hours and both Taylor and Autumn were fired. Taylor quickly found a job at Applebee's. He suggested that Autumn join him there waiting tables. This was her first job as a waitress, so she was nervous about trying it. Little did she know that she would blossom like a social butterfly. She was now putting her great personality and people skills to use, adding to that, her great smile. She was making good money and she was networking with influential people. Life was good.

Autumn would work from 3pm until 2:30am in the morning. After work she would go out drinking with Taylor, his twin brother Turner and some co-workers. Taylor had a friend who managed a local bar across from Applebee's and his friend would serve the Applebee's crew drinks on the house. Sometimes they drank until the sun came up.

~

Autumn and Taylor graduated at the top of their classes. They were proud of each other. Taylor's parents threw him a graduation party while Aleyah only gave Autumn a card before walking out of the door with one of her male friends. As usual, Autumn felt alone; she had just graduated from high school, something neither of her parents had done, but, neither Aleyah nor Mike were emotionally available to celebrate in their daughter's achievement. She was upset that she couldn't enjoy her accomplishment with her family. True, she had Taylor and her co-workers, but, deep down this was a moment she wanted to share with her parents.

The summer after graduation was crazy. Aleyah got a puppy, something that was against the apartment's policy. Autumn knew this was against the rules and feared that they would be evicted, her mother on the other hand, had no worries. Just their luck, one of the neighbors heard the dog barking and reported it. Aleyah was given a warning, but would not get rid of the dog.

Autumn's fear had come true; since her mother refused to get rid of the dog, they had to vacate the premises immediately, and had no place to go. They packed their stuff in the car and drove around trying to figure out where they would be sleeping that night.

They started out at Kenya's house. Kenya was a longtime friend of Aleyah's. Kenya's mother Linda and Aleyah's mother had been best-friends for over 40 years, so Kenya and Aleyah had basically grown up together. Kenya and her daughter Amani lived together. Amani was Autumns' age so they got along pretty well.

Aleyah and the girls stayed with Kenya and Amani for two weeks before they hopped to another house. This time they stayed with one of Aleyah's co-workers named Anne. She lived in a two-bedroom home, which was built for two people, not four. That lasted a week before Anne grew tired of her space being invaded and put them out. At that point there was nowhere else for them to go, so they lived in their car and hotels when Aleyah could afford them.

Thankfully, Aleyah found another apartment two months later. Autumn was so grateful to God because she couldn't take another night of sleeping in the car. She had gained a new respect for the homeless.

They moved into a new place around the corner from Kenya and Amani. Once they were settled, they began attending a church around the way. The Pastor and his ministry team were good people and had great energy. They showed lots of love to their members. They built personal relationships, showed affection, and prayed for families who desperately needed it.

Aleyah and the girls would attend church five days out of the week and things were going great. The energy in this church was nothing short of amazing and Autumn felt as if she had finally found a church where she belonged. The word had never been clearer to her. Autumn and the other church members especially loved the praise team who sang their hearts out. The praise and worship was awesome and very moving. Autumn had never felt this way before.

Autumn decided to join the Praise Dance team. Dancing for the Lord was a new way to express the joy of the Holy Ghost and she took great pride in expressing her love for the Lord.

Autumn began to do a complete 180. She stopped listening to questionable music, watching television, smoking weed, and even changed the company that she kept. She had become a "Christian girl."

Her drastic change began to take a toll on her relationship with Taylor. He wasn't ready to fully commit himself to the Lord and he started to change towards her. Autumn was learning as much as she could about seeking her spiritual growth. She was reading the Bible almost every day, and for the first time she actually understood what she was reading. She was raised in the church and never understood the word until now. God had Autumn's full attention, maybe now because she was a little older and the word had been given in a format that she could understand. She quickly learned that once the "Super Connection" with God is in place, everything else that's not good for you starts to fade away.

Taylor started to become distant and at first it didn't dawn on her, but it soon became evident. As she set out on a journey to soul restoration, she became a lot more comfortable in her skin and her true spirituality began to peak.

One Sunday afternoon they attended a second service at church. Autumn's soul was lifted in the most amazing way and she felt inspired to participate in the Testimonial part of the service. For the first time in her life she didn't feel ashamed about sharing her abuse, although this time it would be in front of a crowd. As she stood up to begin her road to redemption her heart began to race as she told the story of how she had been violated in the worst way.

Eyebrows began to rise, and some people seemed surprised. When she began speaking, some were paying attention, but once she got into the story, everyone had her full attention as she shared her piece of hell on earth. She fumbled with her words, feeling like a young child again, ashamed and unworthy. Her eyes were on the floor as she continued to talk. "It wasn't your fault honey," Yelled a voice in the crowd. "Praise God!"

"When I was eight years old, I was molested, raped and beaten by a man that my family had known and trusted for over twenty years. He was so close that he almost married my mother. The devil is so sneaky, he'll be right up under your nose, if you don't pay attention."

Aleyah sat next to her daughter filled with shame, she had to accept the fact that she was to blame for her Autumns abuse, yet she would never admit to it.

Autumn cried and shouted so hard after that demon was released. She felt as if a huge burden had been lifted from her shoulders. Her heart had been cleansed and everyone was shouting in the Holy Spirit along with her. After everyone calmed down, hugs and joyous kisses were shared. There was one thing that unnerved Autumn however, Pastor Henry hadn't come to console her. This was out of character for him considering that he always came to share love after the service. Autumn was looking forward to hearing from him more than anyone else that evening but something was not right and she was going to find out exactly what it was.

When they left church Autumn felt that there were still some unanswered questions. Both Aleyah and her daughter were shocked at Pastor Henry's behavior.
"Did you notice that Pastor Henry didn't even come by to say hello as usual?" asked Aleyah.
"Yes, I noticed. That was weird, he always comes by to show some type of love." Said Aleyah.
 This stayed on Autumn's mind for the entire week.

The following Wednesday they went to church for bible study. Again, Pastor Henry was distant, he only waved at them from the pulpit. Autumn thought something was seriously out of place. Then on Friday when Autumn went to work a few of her co-workers told her the harsh truth. "You know that your pastor was on TV right?" "For what?" Asked Autumn.

"He was on the news. They say that he was molesting little boys." Autumn was beyond shocked and appalled.

"What are you talking about? There is no way that could be true!"

All of sudden, she felt overwhelmed as several voices began speaking to her. They revealed that her Pastor, the one who helped her to understand her spirituality had been abusing children. "Oh lord!"

Autumn immediately started to have a panic attack. First, she needed to find out if this could possibly be the truth. Secondly, how would she handle such a thing if it were in fact true? She had put so much trust in this man. *'Damn!'* She thought to herself as she ran to call her mother to see if she had heard anything about this. Like Autumn, she too was shocked and now they both were feeling uneasy.

When she got off work that evening, she and Aleyah watched the news and sure enough there he was. He had on one of his best suits and was answering questions about allegations that he had been sexually abusing young boys and bribing them with gifts, money, and clothes.

Autumn was disappointed, hurt, disgusted and confused. *'What the hell is going on in this crooked world to make a man of God commit such a cruel act upon a child and have the audacity to get in the pulpit all week and preach to a crowded church on how to live right?'*

This was insane and now Autumn realized that no one was perfect and that all people made mistakes. This even applied for those who preached the word of God. Some lines however should never be crossed, and Pastor Henry went so far past the line that the line was no longer visible.

The next day there was a church meeting called to address the allegations Pastor Henry was facing. About one fourth of the members showed up, and of course most of them did not believe a word that had been said. Autumn went because she needed some kind of clarification at this point, she was in denial. She could not fathom how this man of God, a man who would take all of the young men out and have a guy's night, give them nice clothes, shoes, etc. for good grades, could possibly do something like this. Autumn had learned in her past experiences not to put anything past anyone.

Another red flag was raised; Pastor Henry had a family, a wife and a son who was only a year old. So many questions were floating around in her head, *'Does his wife know about this? How did his wife feel when she found out that her husband was a child molester who liked boys? How would this affect his marriage? How would this affect his son? And most importantly, how would this affect the church?'*

Her brain was all over the place. Everyone had questions. Some gave their opinions about the situation and discussed what would be best going forward as members of the church. A few were adamant about having the Pastor's back, they felt that there was no way that he could have committed such a crime. As the meeting continued Pastor called the church and was put on the loud speaker.

"Hello Family!" He said with much confidence and sternness in his voice. Some said hello, others just sat there. "I can't express the hurt and disappointment that I feel as I'm sure you all are feeling. You know that when the devil sees a good thing going he has to come in and set some traps. We will not allow him to defeat us, we are more than conquerors! The devil is a liar! Just hold on and have faith in God, and in me. Don't allow the devil to take what we've built and destroy it. You all know that I did no such thing. I am a man of God! So, when that garbage comes on your television, turn it off! Don't even feed the fire, just know that your Pastor is innocent!"

It was as if this man was running a campaign. If this were the case he would have won the election. Most of the faces in the room were sold and shouting out "Amen! Hallelujah!" There were people speaking in tongues, praying and crying. Autumn was still confused though. She was torn between the old eight-year-old girl who had been violated and her new spiritual beliefs. She was at a standstill. It was like crossing a train track and getting your shoe caught on the track with the train barreling straight toward you. The decision was hard either way. Save your life and walk home with one bare foot, or keep on your shoe and lose your life. Autumn just couldn't abandon the fact that Pastor Henry could have taken away a child's innocence, the way someone had taken hers away.

Chapter 29
The Snowball Effect

Taylor and Autumn began to drift apart and Autumn was deep in denial, she just couldn't see it. Taylor began taking an interest in one of their co-workers Maria. She was Latin with long jet-black hair. At the time Maria was going through a messy break-up with her boyfriend. She came to Autumn for consoling because she had developed a closeness with her over the past several months. Autumn felt bad for Maria so she would invite her to hang out with Taylor and herself to keep Maria from being lonely.

Autumn's kindness quickly came back to haunt her. Soon after, Taylor was spending more time trying to heal Maria's broken heart than he was with her. His demeanor towards Autumn had completely changed. He had become nonchalant and distant in their conversations, disregarding her feelings and flirting with women in her face. Autumn wanted to gain back leverage in the relationship, so she decided to break up with him. That turned out to be a very bad move…

The following Sunday, Autumn went to church alone. Every time the church doors opened, she looked back, hoping that Taylor would walk in. She thought that if they prayed together all would be well. Taylor never showed up, and as the service went on, her heart sank more and more with each passing moment. When service was over she checked her phone to see if he had called to apologize, or just because he was thinking of her, but there was nothing. On the ride home she was silent, wondering what she would do if he didn't come back.

When Autumn got home, she went straight upstairs to her room and dialed his number. Her heart was racing with every breath she took. After two rings, he answered. "Hello," he said.

Autumn took a deep breath. "Hey, it's me. We should talk."

"You're right," Taylor said.

"What is going on with us?"

"You broke up with me Autumn, remember?"

"Of course I remember, I was upset, not to mention hurt because you've been distant and flirting with other girls in my face. That is so unlike you. Please, tell me what is going on."

"I really can't explain it, things are just different."

"What do you mean?" She questioned. He was silent. "Do you still love me?"

"Yes, I still love you Autumn."

"Then, what is wrong? Is there someone else?"

"Yes."

Autumn was silent as her heart fell to her feet. "Who is she? When did this happen? We just broke up!"

"I'm not dating anyone, but I am interested in someone."

"How can you do this when you just told me that you love me?"

"I do love you, I'm just not in love with you anymore." He confessed.

Those words pierced the depths of her soul. She lost complete control as her body started to meltdown. Her heart was on fire and her body was totally numb from the head to toe. She couldn't hold the phone any longer and there was no feeling left inside of her body as she slid onto the floor. Just when she thought that it couldn't get any worse, she started wondering who took her place. *'Maria? If this bitch...'* Autumn wanted to ask, but she knew she couldn't handle the answer at that moment, instead she hung up the phone.

Drowning in her pain, she couldn't eat, sleep, or function for the first week - she wouldn't even get out of the bed. She didn't want to see sunlight and couldn't watch television because everything she saw reminded her of Taylor. Every time she tried or even thought about eating she vomited. Autumn was fading away quickly, she literally lost 18 pounds within two weeks. When she finally returned to work things were crazy, she was now faced with the challenge of working face-to-face with the both of them.

Maria immediately sensed tension between herself and Autumn, so she approached Autumn.
"Is everything ok?" She asked. Autumn gave her a cold sarcastic stare. "I thought that you were my friend."
Maria looked confused. "I am your friend. What are you talking about?" Again, Autumn gave her a cold stare. Maria just gave a blank look.

"Taylor and I just broke up and I know that you guys have a thing for each other. I just ask that you respect me by not flaunting your relationship in my face."

"Oh my goodness, I didn't know," She said in her Panamanian accent. "Why would you think that I would do something like that to you? You are my girl. Good people are hard to come by and you are good people. Taylor and I are friends but I guarantee you that it will not go any further than that."

Autumn was felt comfortable with her answer and let it go.

A few weeks went by and Taylor and Autumn had not seen each other. He had even adjusted his schedule so that they didn't work together. This was both an advantage and disadvantage. On one hand, she wouldn't have to see him gawking all over Maria, but on the other hand, she wouldn't have a chance to win him back either. This brought on a whole new level of depression.

Autumn was staying at Giselle's house when he finally decided to call a few weeks later. She was excited and nervous at the same time. Finally she would have a chance to get her man back. "Hi," he said. "Hello Taylor."

They both shared an awkward chuckle. "I want to come by and see you, if that's ok?" Autumn's heart skipped a beat. "Sure, that would be nice. I'm at Giselle's."

When they hung up, she didn't know what to think or expect, but she wanted to make everything right between them. When he arrived, things were a little odd, but they managed to work through it. They watched a movie, laughed a bit and then made love. As they were rocking and rolling, he whispered in her ear how much he loved her and asked that she give him some time to clear his mind.

It was obvious that someone influenced him into giving their relationship another chance. Autumn agreed to give Taylor his space and as long as he came back, she believed everything would be fine.

A few days later, Autumn was in Sunday service when she saw Taylor walk in. Her heart immediately fell to her toes and all she could say was, "Thank You Jesus!" She knew that Jesus would bring him back.

Taylor was late though, so he and his friend Craig sat in the back. When service was over he came over to say hello and after they talked, he and Craig took Autumn back to Giselle's house. The ride was very awkward. She just couldn't put her finger on it, but Autumn knew things would not be the same.

A few hours later Craig called Autumn. He wanted to come by to talk, so she gave him permission to stop by. Autumn was curious as to why Craig wanted to talk to her, she knew something was up because Craig had never called her cell before now. When Craig arrived they sat outside and he gave her the run down on how Taylor was making his move on Maria.

"How do you know this?" She asked.

"When we left you earlier, we stopped to pick up some flowers for her." He said bluntly.

Autumn's heart literally stopped and it was hard for her to take another breath. "She told me that she was not going to do this.

She said that she wouldn't date him." She whispered. "She claimed that he was not her type."

Craig sat there shaking his head. He seemed to be in as much shock and pain as Autumn. "She's lying," he said. "They've been hanging out a lot lately."

Autumn was stunned. "Are you serious? That lying, trifling bitch! I should have known better than to trust her! She's nothing but a gold digger! That bitch is going to run circles around that boy."

Craig nodded his head in agreement. "I tried to warn him of the kind of woman she was but you know as well as anyone that people have to figure things out for themselves." said Craig.

He continued telling Autumn that he and Taylor had been hanging out at Maria's house for the past several weeks. Autumn was sick. She knew that she had lost him for good and now all that was left for her to do was to deal with it. This was hard, she didn't want to accept this, merely because she had hoped that Taylor wouldn't hurt her like all the other men in her life.

It had been confirmed Maria had stolen her man, right from under her nose. *'How could I have let this happen?'* She thought.

Autumn's mind went in a million different directions. Her broken heart was lying on the highway in the middle of 5 o' clock traffic, with car after car running right over it.

A few days after receiving the gut wrenching news, Autumn was face-to-face with Maria at work. Of course she and Taylor weren't on the same shift but he did however, make it his business to come visit Maria as the work shift was coming to an end. When Autumn saw him come into the door she immediately grew nauseous and hid so that no one could see the pain on her face. She watched as he walked to Maria with so much excitement and grabbed her hands while he looked into her eyes with infatuation. Autumn's heart began to disintegrate into dust. *'If anyone would have ever explained to me that heartbreak would feel like this, I would have never considered being in a relationship!'* She thought.

Soon, she had become the talk of Applebee's and was the silly young girl who got her man taken away by the Latina Gold digger.

One day as Autumn was finishing her shift, the store manager called her into his office. "What is going on with you?" He asked. "I heard about your break up and I'm sorry, but baby you win some and you lose some. And to tell you the truth, it's his loss, not yours! Let this thing go because all this drama in the work place is very unprofessional. Not to mention, you're letting everyone know that you're hurt. Never wear your emotions on your sleeve. People tend to mistake it for weakness and weakness is not something that I see in you. Plus you have that scary heifer afraid to come to work. You're messing with my schedule."

They laughed and Autumn apologized for her unprofessionalism. He was right and she knew it, She left his office feeling better.

As soon as she set foot on the floor, however, the drama started. "I heard that you've been going around telling people that you were going to smash my face with a hot skillet," said Maria.

Autumn looked her straight in the eye with a smirk on her face, "Yes I said it! I can't stand to look at your trifling ass! You broke the code bitch. You're never to go after a man that a friend of yours is dating - that gives me grounds to kick your ass!"

"I'm not even dating him, I told you that already. He and I are only friends." Said Maria

"Well, that's not what I heard." Snapped Autumn. "I know that he's been at your house hanging out lately. One thing that I can't stand is a person who can look you straight in the eyes and lie!"

Maria turned and stormed off. Autumn's first thought was to yank her by the hair and beat her down right there, but decided against it, she wasn't worth the trouble.

Chapter 30
A Woman Scorned - The Get Over It Process

Autumn finally received a response from Georgia State University. She was accepted and due to start in the fall. Because of the drama with Taylor, she couldn't seem to find the joy in the news. As the weeks went on, she grew more and more unstable, her mind and heart were on a mission to get even.

Autumn's mind began to grow devious, every day she would think of ways she could sabotage Taylor and Maria's relationship. She wanted to make their lives a living hell. She spent days upon days plotting schemes. Most nights were sleepless as she wallowed in pain, desperately wanting to get past the agony, but just couldn't seem to shake it. After some long drawn out thought, she came up with a plan. She had often heard her mother say that to get over a man, just get under a new one. She began thinking of who she could call to occupy her time. Autumn had not eaten properly in weeks and she was also working a hectic schedule. Despite those facts, her figure was still tight. She knew it was time for her to get back in the game - she was young, beautiful and a soon to be a college student. There was no reason she should be depressed over a guy. Her new motto was "On to the next!" She realized that she shouldn't have been in a committed relationship at such a young age anyway. One of the lessons she learned was that *she* should live her life. There would be plenty of time to fall in love. Autumn decided to explore her options and test the waters before settling.

Time definitely had opened her eyes to things she was once oblivious to.

The good thing about working for Applebee's is that it was such a great networking spot where you could meet all kinds of people there. It's a restaurant that doubles as a sports bar and celebrities would come through at any time of the day. Autumn met, Jadakiss, Andre 3000, Big Boi, and Johnny Gill. She also met a girl named April while working there.

April was a country girl bursting with personality, she was very blunt, but fun. She knew all the hot spots in Atlanta and was excited about showing Autumn the city. She took Autumn uptown to the heart of Atlanta, showing her the famous Buckhead strip. It was where everyone was and where everyone wanted to be. There were miles of clubs, bars and restaurants. Some of the more popular spots were the Cheesecake Factory, ESPN sports bar and Copeland's. On the opposite side were the four blocks of night clubs. The Tounge & Groove, World Bar, Havanna Club, and Visions were very popular.

April had a car and lots of sexy clothes and shoes. Another thing she had was game; she had a lot of connections and knew security guards at just about every club and could get into all of the hot spots for free. Autumn and April would be dressed to kill - miniskirts and heels were the norm. They would smile, hug the guards and waltz right in the club, it worked every time. Autumn loved hanging with April not only did she know the guards, she also knew the bartenders and it was oooon! They would drink free all night and dance on the stage.

They loved being in the spotlight. ATL had Autumn WIDE OPEN!

The girls would work hard during the week and play hard on the weekends. They were regulars in the Buckhead scene. Autumn's favorite spot became the World Bar. She loved the layout, plus they had a stage in the center of the club where she would dance all night. After partying like rock stars, they would hit up Ihop and then drag themselves into bed right before the sun came up only to do it all again…

Autumn was having a ball and things were finally starting to get better. Taylor had become non-existent in her mind. But it was time for Autumn to get laid, she needed to feel someone inside of her. Who would be her rebound victim? April and Autumn would sometimes chat about getting laid. During one of their conversations, April told her about her exciting sex life, sharing that she was bi-sexual. Now Autumn had, had a few escapades, but nothing quite like that. She knew nothing about it but was intrigued, so decided to ask for details. "What does bi-sexual mean exactly?" Autumn asked.

"It's when you like both men and women," April explained.

"Really? So, you've had sex with a woman before?"

"Yes, and it was amazing!"

Autumn sat across from April with her mouth wide open, her mind was wandering all over the place. "So, how do two women have sex?"

"We perform oral sex on each other, kissing and licking each other's breast. Once, a girl used a "strap-on" on me then I did it to her. And depending on how freaky you really are, you can grind clits."

Autumn's mouth was still wide open, she had never heard anything like this before. She knew of lesbians, but never cared enough to find out how they got down. This was interesting and definitely had her a little curious.

April then gave Autumn a look she had never seen. "So, what do you think about everything I just said?"

"I'm blown away! This is definitely one of the most interesting conversations that I've ever had."

April giggled, "So would you be interested in having a threesome?"

Again, Autumn was speechless. At this point, she was so nervous she began stuttering. "I-I'm not into girls."

"Let me be your first then, I'll teach you all about it. You'll enjoy the experience, I promise." April said with a sinister smile.

"I'm just not ready for that." Autumn replied. "I don't go down on girls. The thought of my face in another girl's bush is a little disturbing." She said with her face tooted up as if there were a stench of stink in the air.

"I'll just go down on you. You can just lay back and enjoy it." Said April.

"I don't know about that April, it just sounds weird. Let me get back to you about it."

"All right, that's cool."

Autumn left the table feeling weird. She couldn't believe her girl had just made a pass at her.

Several new hires had come into Applebee's and April had become friends with one of the new girls. This was great for Autumn because she wanted to avoid her at all costs. Their freaky conversation a few weeks earlier was too much. Autumn soon grew bored and missed the exciting times she and April shared. Bored, she called April to see what she had on her agenda for the weekend. April had plans to go to a strip club and invited Autumn to come along. Being new to the nightlife in Atlanta, Autumn was skeptical about going, but she decided to go.

The girls made plans to go to Strokers and she was nervous about going to the strip club for the first time because she didn't know what to expect. Atlanta is well known for its strip clubs and nightclubs so Autumn decided that she would enjoy the new experience. She would also be able to finally say that she had gone to a strip club.

When they pulled into the Strokers parking lot there was barely any place to park and Autumn's heart was racing. As they walked into the club, there were lights flashing, men everywhere, and butt naked girls all over the place. Autumn had never seen anything like this, so she didn't know how to act.

One thing she did enjoy about the strip club was that there were men everywhere, and they were spending money. It was like a buffet of men: working class, hustlers, lames, thugs, etc. April looked over and asked, "are you alright Autumn?"

"Yes, I'm fine. Damn, it's like a man buffet up in here." They burst into laughter.
"Do you want a drink?"
"Hell yeah! I could use a drink." She replied.

As they walked to the bar, they definitely caught the attention of several guys. Autumn was eye flirting her ass off. Two guys finally approached them and offered to buy their drinks and the girls gladly accepted, found a seat and began watching the show. There were girls with crazy sexy outfits and tattoos, climbing the poles and doing amazing tricks with their asses. Autumn was like a kid at the circus for the first time. She was amazed and intrigued.

The guys sitting next to Autumn and April were getting lap dances. The strippers were topless, rubbing their titties all up in their faces. Some were bent over and completely naked, making their asses clap while the guys were smacking their ass with stacks of money.

In the corner, near the pool tables, were a group of butch lesbians. One had a stripper by the hair, pulling her back and forth onto her, as if she was hitting it from the back. Autumn was tripping out. *'This is wild as hell!'* she thought. Autumn couldn't hate though, these girls were getting big money.

At the end of the night April and Autumn were pissy drunk. She was nervous on the drive home, hoping that April wouldn't bring up the threesome that she asked about a few weeks ago. "So, did you have fun tonight?" She asked Autumn.

"Yes, that was crazy! I've never been to a strip club before, I was highly entertained to say the least and I'm crazy drunk."

"Me too girl, I'm so drunk, I'm not sure that I'll make it to your house and be able to drive home. Do you mind staying at my house until the morning?" asked April.

"Yeah, that's cool. I'm in no condition to drive either." Autumn confessed.

They pulled up to April's place around 4am and stumbled in the door laughing. "Shit, I'm sorry, let me chill. I don't want to wake your parents." Said Autumn

"Girl, I live alone, there ain't nobody here but us." April grabbed her phone and began texting while Autumn went to use the bathroom. "Damn girl, your place is banging! I love the layout." said Autumn

"Thanks, I work hard to enjoy my freedom. I love having the space to do whatever I want."

"I feel you, I can't wait until I get my own place."

"Yes, there's nothing like having your own freedom. Let's take one more shot before we go to bed." said April

"Ok cool, I'm down."

April walked over to her counter and poured two shots of tequila. "Speaking of BANGING, Autumn you have a banging ass body baby girl. I can't take my eyes off of you."

Before Autumn could respond, there was a knock at the door. "Oh, that's my boo. I hope you don't mind."

Autumn was scared shitless, but kept her cool.

"No, do your thing girl."

April opened the door to a gorgeous man who stood 6 foot 2, with a chiseled body and wavy brown hair. "Brian," said April.

"This is my friend Autumn, Autumn this is Brian."

"Nice to meet you Brian."

"Likewise. Baby you didn't tell me that your girl was such a hottie."

"I was just telling Autumn how banging her body is… Would you like a drink baby?"

"Yeah, I need one."

Brian threw his double shot back like it was nothing. Then he picked April up and kissed her passionately. They began taking off each other's clothes right in front of Autumn. She sat there in shock and nervous as hell, but she couldn't look away. After April's clothes were off Brian laid her down and started eating her pussy. She moaned in ecstasy. Autumns' pussy started to tingle, it had been a while since she got laid. She imagined that she was getting her pussy ate.

After Brian finished eating April he flipped her over doggy-style and started hitting it from the back. They both were staring at Autumn, who was still watching them, with her legs spread across the chair while rubbing her pussy. "Autumn baby, do you like what you see?" asked April. Autumn couldn't say a word - she was turned on, but scared to death. "Come here baby, let me please you," said April. She flicked her tongue out, revealing her tongue ring. And that made Autumn's pussy thump in her panties. She slowly walked toward them and sat on the couch next to them.

While still getting fucked from the back, April undressed Autumn then pulled her in closer. When Autumn was close enough April began licking her nipples. Brian was super excited when he got a glimpse of Autumn's naked body. "Mmmm, I like that, let me see you eat that pussy," he said. "Whatever you like daddy!" April gently moved from Autumn's breast to her pussy and burst her bi-sexual cherry. She moaned with pleasure as April went to work on her pussy, all while Brian was still fucking her. So many emotions were running through her head. She thought to herself how amazing it felt and knew it was wrong, but she liked it, so she figured she might as well enjoy it. "D-Damn baby this pussy is super sweet. I could eat it all day long." Purred April.

"Mmmm, can I taste it baby?" Asked Brian.

"Sure baby, if she doesn't mind."

"Hell no, I don't mind!" Autumn blurted out.

Brian dove deep in her pussy and had her moaning even louder. April joined him, licking the clit while he tongue fucked her. Autumn was in over her head, but she couldn't stop them, it felt too good. She exploded, and they both sucked the cum out of her. Brian then turned the heat up by putting Autumn on all fours. He then placed April on top of her and had both girls bent over. He stuck his dick in Autumn and his tongue in April. They were all so wet and sticky... Both girls moaned until they all came in unison. They hit the shower then fell straight to sleep. On her way to sleep Autumn's only thought was *Taylor who?*

Chapter 31
Pain Meets Love

A week later, Autumn awoke around 6am to get ready for class. She had to be alert and focused if she was going survive college life. Majoring in psychology and maintaining a 4.0 grade point average would be difficult, but she was on a mission and wasn't going to allow anything to get in her way. Today her mind was cloudy, she couldn't shake the dream she had about her dad's sister Charmaine. Charmaine and Autumn were very close, so she could feel when something was wrong with her favorite aunt. Autumn decided that she would give her a call once her busy day calmed. She had a full day ahead of her with three classes and work.

Autumn decided to transfer to a more popular Applebee's where she could make a guaranteed $600 dollars a week and not have to worry about running into Taylor or Maria. She needed to stay focused on her studies and work to make up the money to pay for tuition, so moving from a hostile environment to get her priorities in order was a must.

As her shift was ending, Autumn received a call from her mother. "Hey, how much longer will it be before you make it home?" "I'm walking out now. What's wrong?"

Autumn could hear the pain in her mother's voice. "I'd rather discuss it when you get home."

"Ok, I'll be home in 45 minutes."

Her thoughts automatically shot to her dream and the feelings that consumed her for the first part of the day.

When Autumn walked through the door, her mother and Naomi were sitting on the couch crying. Her heart started racing. "What happened? Why are you guys crying?"

Aleyah choked up as she tried to find the words, "Charmaine is in the hospital."

Autumn immediately became light headed and nauseous. Tears were rolling down her face. "What happened to her?"

"She was coming out of a bar. Some young guys were arguing and they began shooting at each other. Charmaine got caught in the cross fire."

Her body felt hot all over "Oh My Gosh!"
"Is she going to be all right?"
"They're not sure. She's in the ICU fighting for her life."

Autumn went into her bedroom to process the news. Her heart was heavy and the tears wouldn't stop flowing. The only thing she could do was pray. She couldn't shake the thought of her aunt lying in that hospital bed. She called her grandmother back home to check on the status. Grandma Lola told Autumn that Charmaine was ok and not to worry. Then she asked if Autumn had spoken with her father. Autumn told her that she had been trying to get in touch with him for months, but had not been able to reach him. Once again, Lola told her not to worry, because Mike would turn up soon.

The next day, Autumn received a phone call from Amani. "Hey girl, what's up?" "Hey Amani! Nothing much just chilling at home, what's up with you?"

"I just got my first car, do you want to go for a ride?"

"Congratulations! Sure, I'll ride. I need to get out of this house anyway."

"Cool, I don't know where we're going, but I'm ready to ride out," said Amani.

"Girl, it doesn't matter if we ride to the corner store, I'm ready." They busted out with laughter.

"All right, I'm on the way."

When she pulled up, Autumn was already outside waiting. When she got in Amani asked "You smoke weed?"

"Hell yeah! This is just what I need. I have so much shit going on."

The girls had an instant connection. Amani and Autumn rode around the city smoking, laughing and talking. Autumn was glad she finally had the opportunity to get to know Amani better. She felt comfortable around her, she could be herself. They didn't really have a chance to get to know each other in the short period of time when they lived with her and Kenya.

Later that evening Amani dropped Autumn off at home. When she opened the door Aleyah was crying hysterically.
"Mom, what's wrong?" She asked. Her mother didn't say a word. She just kept crying.

"Please don't tell me that she's gone. Please don't." She begged.

"They found Lola dead on the side of her house a few hours ago." Her mother finally sobbed. "What do you mean? "You're telling me that my grandmother is dead and my aunt is in the hospital fighting for her life?" Autumn passed out.

A few days later they flew back home to Buffalo. When they arrived at Grandma Lola's house, there were people everywhere. Family they hadn't seen in years were there and with each step they took toward the house, Autumn's feet felt heavier. She went inside to find her great aunts looking at photos of Charmaine and Lola. She couldn't find the words to say. She approached them with a forced smile and one of her aunts rose from her seat to give her a hug. After a little chit-chat they walked outside to get some air. "How are you?" Autumn asked.

"I'm dealing," said her aunt. "Now, why don't you go over and say hello to your father."

"My father is here? I haven't seen him."

"You know that he was not going to miss his mother's funeral. They were so close. Go check on him, he needs you right now."

Autumn looked around and couldn't spot her father out of the crowd. She looked back over towards her great aunt as she pointed in his direction. Autumn walked over to where he was standing. His back was facing her and when he turned around, her heart stopped. He was literally skin and bones. He was so skinny that she hardly recognized him. She immediately started to cry. "Hi dad."

He gave her a good long tight hug. There was a look of relief on his face. "Hey sweetheart, how are you?"

"I'm holding up. How are you?"

"Don't worry about me. I'll be just fine."

Autumn and her father spent the rest of the evening catching up. They hadn't spoken in over three years. Mike told her about his stay in Las Vegas. He had ventured off to Sin city and got caught up in the gambling and drug life. He lost all of his money, along with his mind. He shared how he'd planned to hit the jackpot big in Las Vegas with his lucky gambling streak and retire. Things didn't quite work out that way though. Instead, he lost everything he owned and was forced to sleep under palm trees for shelter.

He went on to explain how he had eaten from garbage cans, when he did have an appetite for food, which was rare. He mostly spent his time doing odd jobs in order to satisfy his coke habit. Mike had coke for breakfast, lunch and dinner. It was evident that God protected him because there was no other explanation as to how he had survived during the last several years.

The following morning it rained heavily. Charmaine didn't make it through the night, her liver was too weak to survive the shooting. The entire family was devastated with having two murders within a week. The story about Lola had finally hit the surface. She had been robbed and thrown from her second story window. A neighbor found her naked body on the side of the house.

The family gathered at Lola's home on the day of Charmaine's and Lola's funeral. Everyone was dressed in black. They held hands for prayer before they piled into their cars to begin a painful ride. When they arrived at the church, people were everywhere. Autumns' heart stopped when she saw her first love Chase standing there with a bouquet of flowers. He rushed to her and wrapped his arms around her tightly. After all the years that had gone by, they were still madly in love with each other. Chase had gone out of his way to keep in contact with Autumn once she moved to

Atlanta. He would call to check up on her every now and again, but this was the first time they had seen each other since she moved. Chase was stunned at how beautiful Autumn had grown up to be. She was still also very much attracted to him. He took her hand, kissed it, then walked her into the church.

Autumn tried to smile but the closer they walked toward the casket, the weaker she felt. She couldn't fathom the fact that her aunt and grandmother were lying there lifeless. She wouldn't get a chance to see Charmaine's captivating smile or hear Lola's voice again. Her emotions began to get the best of her. She lost control when she saw them up close. She kept closing her eyes and shaking her head, in hopes that this was all a bad dream.

Autumn went over the deep end when Charmaine's 10-year-old son Charles approached the caskets. He was hugging the casket, screaming for his mom and grandmother to come back. Autumn ran out the room, she just couldn't take the pain. Chase ran behind her. When he caught up to her, he grabbed her and held her tightly. He kissed her forehead as she wept her eyes out. It was as if he took some of the weight from her heavy heart, because she suddenly felt at ease, even if only for the moment.

After the burial everyone met back at Lola's home for dinner and fellowship. Chase was right at Autumn's side. He even sat to eat dinner with them. Afterwards they sat on the porch to catch up on what they had missed over the years. Their conversation lasted until the wee hours of the morning. It was then that they both realized they still loved each other a great deal. Gazing into each other's eyes, they kissed passionately. "Let's go for a ride," he said. "I want to take you somewhere special."

They drove down to the Marina, made love and watched the sun rise.

"You are beautiful Autumn, I've missed you so much." said Chase.

"I've missed you too. I still feel the connection between us. I can't tell you enough how much I appreciate you being by my side." said Autumn.

"I'll always be by your side baby, I love you Autumn."

Her heart dropped to her toes. "I love you too Chase."

Chapter 32

Gone In Sweet November

It was mid-November, several months after Charmaine and Lola had passed and Chase confessed his feelings. Autumn was trying to get back in the swing of things. She had obligations that had to be met. Classes were kicking her ass and working long hours was wearing her out. It was another busy day at Applebee's and Autumn knew that she had to prepare herself mentally because she was sure it was going to be a long day. After she got her section ready, the hostess told her that there was a guest who requested her to be their waitress. She turned on her winning smile and personality then approached the table to introduce herself. There sat a good-looking gentleman in his early 30's, well dressed and he smelled divine.

He was about 6'2, with a light complexion, a nice build, and a clean cut. *'Damn, this dude is fine,'* Autumn thought. And she loved the pretty smile he flashed, she had a definite weakness for men with pretty smiles.

"My name is Deon, I've been watching you for a while now and I couldn't resist the opportunity to get to know you."

Autumn batted her slanted eyes and smiled. "Hi, I'm Autumn, I'll be your waitress. Would you like to start off with a drink?"

"Yes, a rum and coke and your phone number please."

"I'll have your Rum and Coke up shortly. As for giving you my number, that'll be determined by how well you tip."

She winked her eye and walked away. When she returned with his drink, Deon smiled again. Her beauty and confidence seemed to be intriguing to him. She took his order and kept a professional attitude. Autumn had a lot on her mind and meeting another man was not one of them. Her nonchalant attitude was turning him on even more. She could tell he was used to having women melt as soon as he approached them.

Deon was at the end of his meal when Autumn walked back over. "Is there anything else I can get for you this evening?"

"Yes, a chance to take you out." He responded.

They both giggled as she handed him the check. When he placed the money in her hand, there was a neatly folded note. As she went to get his change she slipped the note inside her pocket and continued to work. As soon as she got out of his sight she pulled the note from her pocket:

I can't stop thinking about your smile. Your eyes have me intrigued. Please allow me to take you out. I just want to be in your presence.
-Deon (4) 253-7777

Autumn blushed and bit her bottom lip. She was already daydreaming about what a date with Deon would be like.

She waited a few days before calling, she didn't want to seem too anxious. "Hi Deon, It's Autumn from Applebee's."
"Autumn what's up? I thought that you had forgotten all about me."
"No, I don't think that I could forget such a beautiful smile."

"When will I get a chance to spend some time with you Angel?"

"I'm off this weekend" she said.

"This weekend is perfect! My cousin who plays football for the Baltimore Ravens is throwing a party. Would you like to be my date?"

"Sure! That sounds like fun."

"Cool, I'll pick you up on Friday at 9pm. Afterwards we can grab something to eat. I can't wait to see you."

"Awesome, I'll be ready and dressed to impress!"

Friday couldn't come fast enough. Autumn needed a break from everything. She had just taken a midterm for her Psych class, work was crazy, and she hadn't been laid in months (since her rendezvous with Chase a few months back).

April had been begging to taste Autumn's sweet pussy for the last few weeks. Her schedule had been hectic and she didn't want April getting too attached. The head was good, but Autumn wasn't a lesbian, it was all in fun. As the weekend approached and things began to slow down Autumn's pussy tingled for attention. It was as if April smelled her scent in the air because she called to see if Autumn wanted to have drinks after work. She accepted her invitation and told April to pick her up at midnight.

The girls went to a local bar, shot some pool and went round for round with shots of Patron. By the end of the night they were wasted. April was anxious to leave, she couldn't wait any longer to have Autumn's pussy on her lips. As soon as they got in the car she lifted Autumn's skirt and dove right in. She licked and sucked on Autumn's pussy like a wild woman. Autumn flipped her over and rode April's face until her sweet nectar shot into her mouth. April was a straight up freak, she sucked the cum out of Autumn until there was none left, then began licking it again. This time she stuck her finger in Autumn's pussy, touching her G-spot. Autumn moaned in ecstasy as April turned her over and began licking her ass. Autumn was quite surprised, but she went with it. The combination of the tongue in her ass, a finger in her pussy and other hand tugging at her nipple drove her wild. Autumn thought to herself, *'Damn, this bitch is a freak for real, but I like it! This was just what I needed to relieve my stress.'*

After cuming three times Autumn fell back onto the seat. April climbed onto Autumn and tried to kiss her on the lips, but she turned her head away. "Damn baby, I've fucked a lot of girls but none of them taste like you or drive me crazy the way you do. I can't get you out of my mind" said April.

Autumn didn't say a word. She was still trying to catch her breath, plus there was nothing to say. This arrangement was all in fun. Autumn loved that she could get some head and not return the favor, it worked perfectly. "I think I'm in love with you Autumn."

Autumn sat up straight in her seat. "April, I'm flattered, but I thought we were just having fun. I'm not into girls like that. This is an experimental thing for me, I thought I made that clear. You're my girl and we have fun, but I don't want to be in a relationship with you or any other female, I love men."

"I understand, it's cool. Well, anytime you need that pussy eaten right, don't hesitate to call, I'll come whenever you want me" said April.

April dropped Autumn off at home and she couldn't wait to get out of the car. She thought to herself, *'This bitch is tripping. I can't get down with her like that anymore, she's too clingy for me.'* Her thoughts were interrupted when she saw Niles sitting on the couch. They said hello, then Autumn headed straight to the shower to wash off all the cum between her thighs. Afterwards, she went back downstairs to watch TV. She was still wide-awake and hoped that the TV could help relax her.

She ended up falling asleep on the couch, but was awaken around 6am by Niles' tongue in her pussy. She turned over to give him better access to her sweet hole. Autumn had taught him quite well how to eat it, because he was navigating his way around that thang like a pro. He took two of his fat fingers and entered her pussy as he sucked on her clit gently. Then he cupped her ass and pulled her closer, pushing her legs back by her head and stuck his tongue in her ass. He rocked her back and forth on his tongue. Autumn came hard. She was two for two and didn't even have to return the favor to either of them. She was quite pleased.

Friday night had finally arrived, Deon pulled up in a Midnight blue Lexus. Autumn wore a little black dress that was cut low in the front with the back out and black Victoria Secret stilettos. Deon was standing by the passenger door as she walked to the car. As he opened the car door for her he couldn't stop smiling. "Damn Angel! You look amazing" he said. "Thanks! You look pretty good yourself." "I'm so used to seeing you in your work uniform. I had no idea that you had all those curves, mmm!"

"So, where is the party being held?" said Autumn.

"It's at the downtown Westin Hotel. Have you ever been there before?"

"No, but I'm excited." She smiled.

They arrived at the Westin Hotel. It was a beautiful tall sphere shaped building made of glass. They walked into the lounge where there was a large crowd, fine men were everywhere. She couldn't believe that she was in a room full of ballers. Deon introduced her to his cousin, who was the Quarterback for the Baltimore Ravens, he was even sexier than Deon. OMG! She kept it cool as they shook hands. His cousin told them to head over to the bar, drinks were free all night. Three shots of patron later she was good and tipsy. The music was rocking, so it was time for Autumn to do her thing on the dance floor.

She pulled Deon by the hand and led him to the center of the crowd. She danced slow and sexy in her little black dress. Deon, along with several other men in the room couldn't keep their eyes off her. Autumn was hot and she could feel herself heating up the room. Deon came closer and their bodies began to rock to the beat of the music. He spun her around facing him. They were now so close that she could feel his breath on her lips and his manhood getting excited on her thigh. She smiled and flirted with her eyes. Deon smiled back and kissed her lips with hunger.

She was tipsy and had become totally caught up in the moment. "You are so sexy," said Deon. "And you smell delicious! I'm so honored that you agreed to be my date. Take a look around, all of the men are gawking with envy."

They giggled in unison. Autumn blushed as she took a look around to see all the eyes watching them. "Thank you. You are quite sexy yourself mister."

'This man is fine!' She thought. *'I see the look in his eyes, he wants it. The chemistry between us is hot, but I want him to work for my goodies.'*

It was late and Autumn decided that it was time to leave the party. She didn't want to give Deon the wrong impression. She knew that he was going to try to make his move. "Hey, I'm ready to get out of here, I'm a little tired" she said.

"Cool, I was about to suggest that we head out. Maybe we can grab something to eat, if you are up for it."
"That sounds like a good idea." They left the party and went to the Waffle House. To her surprise Deon was a complete gentleman. They talked about all types of things while eating. He was quite an interesting man. He was 28 and the CEO of several collection agencies. He owned his

home and had four cars. She was impressed and intrigued. She felt that he could definitely be a potential candidate. She really loved the fact that he hadn't attempted to take her home on the first date.

A few weeks had passed and Deon and Autumn had been speaking over the phone and had went on several dates. They were having a great time and Deon still hadn't made a move. His patience turned Autumn on even more. He invited her out for a walk in Centennial Park and she was delighted. It was a beautiful breezy evening, the lights in the park were bright and the air was fresh. Deon held her hand tight as they walked and talked. "I have a confession," he said.

"Ok, say what's on your mind baby?"

"These last few weeks, I've been on a high. You give me this intoxicating feeling, something I cannot explain."

Autumn was speechless as he grabbed her by the waist and kissed her. "I'm flattered, the feeling is mutual," she smiled.

He took hold of her hand. "Follow me," he said. "We have another destination this evening."

Deon blind folded Autumn for the trip to their next venue. When she opened her eyes they were Inside the Marriott Marquis hotel. It was the most spectacular hotel she'd ever seen. It had 50 Floors, 6 restaurants, 1569 rooms, 3 lounges, gifts shops, etc. She was amazed and yet again astonished. They had dinner and a few drinks inside the "Pulse" restaurant.

Once they reached the room, there were candles lit throughout the entire room, rose petals were spread on the bed along with a sexy purple satin gown. The view overlooking the city of Atlanta from the 37th floor was breathtaking. Her eyes grew big as she rushed into his arms and kissed him. "You are a pretty charming guy. Give me 10 minutes to freshen up. I'll be with you shortly."

Autumn went into the bathroom to take a hot shower. As the hot water rolled down her body, she reminisced over the last few weeks and how magical they had been. *'This gorgeous man has been a complete gentleman and has wined and dined me beyond my expectations. I can get used to this royal treatment,'* she thought.

She walked back into the bedroom wet and ready. Deon was lying shirtless on the bed. His body was chiseled like a statue. Music was playing in the background and two glasses of Champagne were in his hands. They shared a smile as she slowly strolled towards him. He handed her a glass and whispered softly, "You are a vision of beauty and I'm going to take my time with you. I want to show you just how much you're worth, my sexy Angel."

Deon's hands smoothly caressed her face, then they kissed slow and passionately. He pulled Autumn on top of him while continuing to plant kisses on all over her face, neck, and breast. She was so aroused and excited that her nipples were erect. He lifted Autumn onto his shoulders with her pussy in his face and ate her sweetness as if it were his last meal. Then, he laid her on her back, placed her legs on his shoulders, and put her toes in his mouth. He sucked her toes, rubbed her clit and entered his manhood, all at the same time.

He stroked her slow and deep. Then he tossed her over onto her hands and knees, planting kisses all over her back as he entered her warm wet walls from behind. They moaned in unison as he went deeper. Deon was massaging her shoulders, smacking her ass, and pulling her hair. He satisfied Autumn's body in its entirety. She was swimming in a sea of ecstasy. Autumn was hooked and she didn't want the sensation to end. After it was over they laid there panting from all the excitement. He pulled her closer and held her until they fell asleep.

The next morning they were awakened by Deon's phone ringing over and over. Each time he sent it to voicemail. Then Autumn's phone began to ring. She didn't recognize the number but answered anyway. "Hello?"

"Are you fucking my husband Deon?!" Yelled a female voice. Autumn quickly hung up.

"Nigga, you're married? This is some bullshit!" Autumn jumped up and threw on her clothes while Deon tried to explain. She completely tuned him out. After she was dressed she grabbed her phone.

"Amani can you come pick me up from the Marriott Marquis downtown? I'll explain when you get here."

Later in the day Deon began calling. Autumn refused to answer so he left a series of voicemails.

VM #1: "Baby, I apologize. Please come have dinner with me, so we can talk this over."

VM #2: "Autumn, please understand that I love you and I never meant to hurt you. Please pick up the phone."

By the 7th message he was drunkenly singing Aaron Hall's song "I miss you" while it played in the background.

By the 12th message, Autumn was tired of the sound of his voice. It made her stomach turn thinking of a man who would disrespect his wife by having an extramarital affair.

She would not deal with that type of betrayal and disloyalty. Those are essential qualities that separated Autumn from the average person. Loyalty, respect and trust were essential. She believed that they were the foundation of any relationship and without them, there were no substantial grounds to carry on. She was completely done with him, so she decided to delete his number.

It was closing time at Applebee's. After Autumn clocked out she headed for the door. As she got in the parking lot she noticed Deon standing there holding flowers. She rolled her eyes and continued to walk toward the bus stop. "Angel, can we please talk?"

"I don't have any time for a liar and a cheat!" Autumn shouted.

"Please hear me out! I promise that I won't need more than a minute to say what I have to say."

"What do you want Deon?"

"You! You are all I think about. You don't understand how you've changed my life. I feel so incomplete without you. Please, give me another chance."

"You can't be serious! You are married. There are no more chances for you! What part of "I don't date married men" don't you understand? What would I have to look forward to? Being your side piece? I don't think so."

"If you take me back, I will leave her and file for a divorce. I just want you Angel! Look me in the eyes and tell me that you don't love me. I'm in love with you and I can't live without you." he pleaded.

She couldn't believe her ears. "Deon, you are insane! I will not take part in breaking up a family. I'm not sure what type of women you are used to dealing with, but I'm not a home wrecker. I believe in Karma and I know that it can be a bitch. No thank you!"

"Well, can we at least make love one last time? Please Angel?" he begged.

"Deon you are pathetic! Take care." She snapped.

Luckily for Autumn the bus was pulling up. As she got on the bus and sat down, Deon stood watching with a dumb look on his face. She shook her head in disbelief. It troubled her that he would even bring up such a deal. *'Men are full of shit!'* She thought. *'I'm taking a break from dating. I need to focus on my degree. I'm going to call up Amani to see if she wants to roll up a blunt!'*

Deon tried contacting Autumn for several months, but he had no luck. His deceit and betrayal toward Autumn and his family drove her to never spoke to him again.

Chapter 33

The Memoirs of Autumn Fall

Dear Diary,

As I conclude my final year of college, I realize that taking psychology as a major was genius. It has been very beneficial in my life. I've learned why I spiraled so out of control through the years.

I developed a wild side early on due to my parent's reckless lifestyle choices. Whether it was gambling, storing drugs in our home, manipulating people, my mother's countless affairs, or my father's drug problem, watching them take those risks as a young child led me to make some of the same questionable decisions as I grew older. Raised in a life of danger and excitement, I soon began my own journey that developed into a natural habit of living on the edge.

Because of my selfish parents who constantly neglected me, I had to develop my sense of independence much earlier than I should have. One thing is for sure, I don't want to end up like my mother by depending on men to take care of me. With that luxury comes a cost, her fee was her daughter's innocence and sanity.

I am also determined to be the opposite of my father, the drug dealer and addict. But, I soon realized that I had too developed an addiction of my own…

My sexual and physical abuse caused me to develop my sexual addiction and a feeling of unworthiness. I was exposed to sex at such a young age, I began to crave it. Soon, sex became my drug anytime I was hurt, disappointed, angry, alone or even happy. It didn't matter that there was no connection or even a possibility of a future relationship, I used sex as a method of relief in order to cope with pain.

I watched my mother with disdain in my eyes as she hopped from man to man. What I now realize is that I followed in her footsteps. I jumped from one man to the next, dumping them when they could no longer fill the void I needed filled. In my latter years, I had become so addicted to sex, I didn't care if a man of woman got me off. As long as I could cum, get up and walk out, I would use them as I had been used as a child.

My parents created an environment of instability, teaching me that it was normal to up and leave without a trace if I didn't like something or someone. Our home was unstable; we never stayed in one house longer than two years because my parents had been mixed up in all kinds of trouble. We would have to relocate or hide out. That meant a new home, a new school and new friends. That's why I could never make real connections with people, because I figured they would only be in my life temporarily. That is the direct cause of my "no strings attached" attitude.

Thank God I continued to pray. God carried me through all of my adversities, in spite of my wrong doings. It was God who blessed me with the drive and ambition to seek out my dreams. Also, I wanted to prove people like Maxwell and Denzel wrong, who hoped I would become a failure.

I am proud to say that I have overcome a lot of hurdles, disappointments and pain in my life, but I've also accomplished my dreams. I've taken all my disadvantages and turned them into advantages. I have learned not to allow my past to define who I am today. I still have a lot of work ahead of me, because I'm just getting started!

The End…For now

www.ingramcontent.com/pod-product-compliance
Lightning Source LLC
Chambersburg PA
CBHW071644090426
42738CB00009B/1420